WAINWRIGHT
IN SCOTLAND

WAINWRIGHT
IN SCOTLAND

with photographs by
DERRY BRABBS

MICHAEL JOSEPH – BBC

CONTENTS

First published in Great Britain by Michael Joseph Ltd
27 Wrights Lane, London W8 5TZ
and BBC Books, a division of BBC Enterprises Ltd
Woodlands, 80 Wood Lane, London W12 0TT
March 1988
Second impression before publication
Third impression June 1988
Fourth impression October 1988
Fifth impression April 1989
Sixth impression June 1990
Seventh impression July 1992

First published in paperback by Mermaid Books June 1990
Second impression July 1992
Third impression October 1994

© Text: The Estate of the late A. Wainwright 1988
© Photographs: Derry Brabbs 1988
© Original line illustrations: Westmorland Gazette

A CIP catalogue record for this book is available from the British
Library

ISBN 0 7181 2901 6 (hardback)
ISBN 0 7181 3409 5 (paperback)

Typeset in 11/13 point Ehrhardt by Ace Filmsetting, Frome, Somerset
Colour reproduction by Technik Ltd, Birkhamstead
Printed and bound in Great Britain by
Butler & Tanner Ltd, Frome and London

ACKNOWLEDGMENTS

I wish to record my thanks to:

Richard Else and his BBC team for making it possible for me to return to many places I thought I would never see again and for ministering to my comforts;

Jenny Dereham of Michael Joseph Ltd for editing the book and overseeing its publication;

Westmorland Gazette for permission to reproduce drawings of which they hold the copyright;

Derry Brabbs for implicitly meeting my wishes in the selection of viewpoints for his camera;

Betty for checking manuscripts and printers' proofs that my failing eyes cannot see clearly, and for looking after me generally;

W. H. Murray for his excellent book on the western Highlands, *The Companion Guide to the West Highlands of Scotland*, which has been my companion and mentor ever since it was published, and the Scottish Mountaineering Club for their helpful publications although I regret their adoption of metres and kilometres instead of feet and miles;

Judy Potter for looking after our seven cats while we were away from home.

FOREWORD

I HAVE AN abiding memory of my first visit to Scotland. I had enjoyed a wonderful week climbing the mountains of Arran, favoured by a succession of sunny days. The year was 1939 and war clouds were darkening the skies over Europe, but in Arran that week there was awareness only of profound peace. I was enchanted by the loveliness of the island, the tranquillity pervading every scene . . . On the morning of departure from Brodick, a group of villagers foregathered on the pier and, as the boat slowly pulled away, sang to the few passengers on deck the old Scottish air 'Will ye no' come back again?'

I was deeply touched by the sad farewell, having formed an emotional attachment to the island during my brief stay and to the kind folk who lived there, and knowing that I was going home to a war that was now inevitable. The song of the villagers haunted me during the years that followed. I longed to go back, but wartime restrictions on travelling made a return impossible. Arran was out of bounds. I dreamed of the romantic charms and unforgettable beauties of the island but could not bring them to life.

In 1946 I went north of the Border again and commenced a series of exploratory visits that has continued to the present day, usually spending two or three weeks there every year. I found Arran to be as idyllic as I remembered, but enthusiasm for the Scottish scenery now took me the length and breadth of the country, travelling by train and MacBrayne's bus services which introduced me to the Highlands and the western seaboard. I was mightily impressed and excited by all I saw, yet well aware from my study of maps that there were many mountain ranges and much wild territory in remote areas not reached by public transport. Having served my apprenticeship as a sightseeing rubberneck, I ventured further afield on foot, walking along the unfrequented glens and climbing the lonely hills from fixed bases; sometimes I undertook long cross-country expeditions.

In the past twenty years, I have had a car and a willing chauffeur at my disposal, and with their help allied to much rough walking and scrambling, I completed an ambition by making a comprehensive survey of all the higher mountains of the mainland and off-shore islands, producing six volumes of pen-and-ink drawings, 451 in number. All my holidays have been spent north of the Border; I have never had a vacation anywhere else, nor wanted to.

Those are my qualifications for daring, as an Englishman, to write this book about the glories of Scotland and especially of the majesty and grandeur of the Highlands and coastal areas. Scots must forgive me. I love their country as they do.

Opposite *Loch Inchard at Rhiconich*
Half-title page *The view north from Stac Polly*
Title page *View from Garva Bridge*
Contents page *Loch Sunart*

ATLANTIC OCEAN

JOHN O'GROATS
Duncansby Head
START

THE ITINERARY
— and detours —

NORTH

SEA

MORAY FIRTH

SCOTLAND

FINISH

NORTH

SEA

EDINBURGH

GLASGOW

ENGLAND

0 Miles 20

KEY TO THE CHAPTER MAPS

A 82
B 970 } Classified roads on the route.

A 82
B 970 } Classified roads not on the route.

Unclassified roads on and off the route.

Poor quality roads.

YH Youth hostel.

▲ Mountain over 4000 ft
▲ „   „   „   3000 ft
△ „   „   „   2000 ft
⬠ „   „   „   1000 ft

Footpaths on the detours are not shown.
For walking in mountainous areas, the use
of small scale maps together with other
suitable equipment is essential for safety.

THE ITINERARY

MOST VISITORS to Scotland intent on seeing the best of the scenery, and especially those coming from over the Border, tend to travel northwards in stages, halting often to view places already familiar or else recommended in guidebooks.

In this book, I have preferred to start my itinerary in the north and travel southwards, the better to link the highlights of the journey in a continuous route, introducing the Highlands more gradually and ending with a glorious climax.

I have assumed that the journey is made in a private car, principally following main motor roads but with many deviations and detours to places of special interest. I have indicated several recommended walks that may be made from parked cars, even reaching a few of the more spectacular mountain summits. But, in essence, it is a journey on wheels into the realms of beauty and grandeur I know so well and love so much.

GAELIC PLACE NAMES

A problem that besets all writers of the Highland scene is the confusion arising from the different spellings of many of the Gaelic place names, especially those of the mountains, where there is inconsistency even in the prefixes. Thus, for example, the simple Ben is also variously spelt as Beinn, Bheinn and Bienne, and Meal (a hill) also appears as Meall, Mheall, Meallan and Maolle; furthermore, the vowels in the names bristle with accents sloping both ways. Accents I have omitted in this book. Mercifully the writer is not concerned with pronunciation.

I have been persuaded by the publishers to adopt the spellings on the latest maps of the Ordnance Survey and where these differ from those previously accepted have done so with reluctance, rebelling only in a few cases of change in long-familiar names. My own preference would be to use the spellings in the excellent Scottish Mountaineering Club guides. I refuse absolutely, however, to insult the noble mountains of Scotland by quoting their altitudes in foreign metres instead of British feet.

I did once suggest a conference of Scottish historians, Gaelic scholars, the Scottish Mountaineering Club and other authorities, with the Ordnance Survey in attendance, to agree once and for all on the correct spelling of Gaelic place names. Nothing happened. For writers, the frustration continues.

A.W.

THE FAR NORTH

THE NORTH coast of Scotland faces the Arctic over a distance of seventy miles and is terminated abruptly by Cape Wrath in the west and Duncansby Head near John o' Groats in the east. John o' Groats is commonly but wrongly regarded as the most northerly tip of the country and because of this popular misconception attracts many visitors, most of whom come for no better reason than to be able to say they have been there and, having satisfied this ambition, turn round and return south. For a few hardier souls, it is the springboard for a 700-mile marathon to Land's End in Cornwall, a destination even more sacrificed to commercial exploitation. Apart from the cliffs and shoreline, there is little here to delay discerning searchers of natural beauty, the hinterland being dreary and desolate, and it is to the west that footsteps and car wheels must turn to find the dramatic scenery and fine landscapes of the far north.

A road, the A.836, leaves John o' Groats and adopts a tortuous course following the fretted coast, and after bypassing Dunnet Head, the most northerly point of the mainland, reaches the pleasant

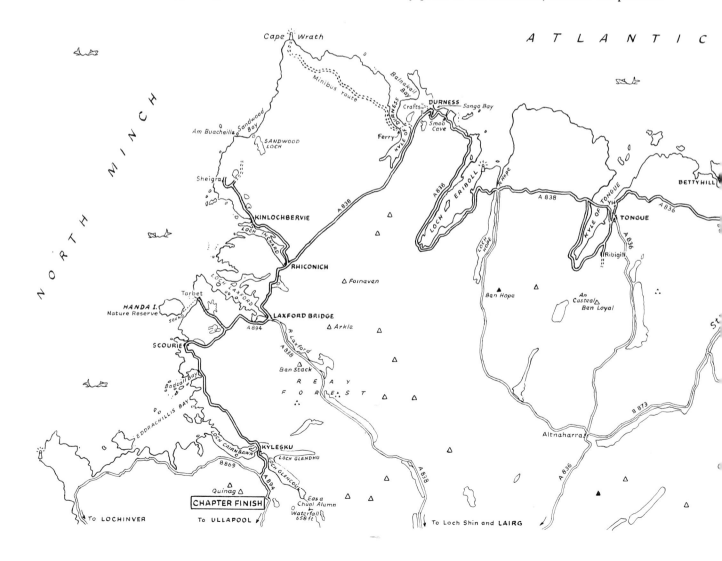

market town of Thurso which has many interesting features deserving a leisurely halt. Beyond the town, the old county boundary is crossed, Caithness being left for Sutherland, both of these ancient counties having now sadly lost their identities in the new-fangled administrative area known as the Highland Region – one hopes that Caithness will for ever remain Caithness and Sutherland Sutherland in the minds of Scotsmen: historical associations should not be trampled on by modern bureaucracy.

The road continues west with little indication of the excitement soon to come, passing through Bettyhill at the foot of Strath Naver, notable for its botany and ancient monuments, and after a detour inland comes alongside the Kyle of Tongue, a sea loch that penetrates deep into the interior. The road, now the A.838, crosses the water by a modern bridge making unnecessary the long detour around the head of the Kyle. This latter alternative, the old route, is strongly to be recommended, however, the traveller being rewarded by a magnificent intimate view of a mountain of rare visual appeal, Ben Loyal, the first of the scenic highlights I have selected for inclusion in this book.

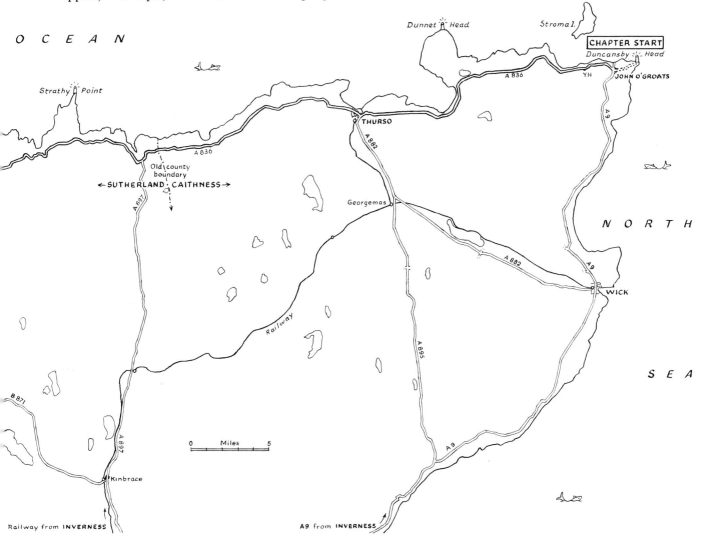

BEN LOYAL

Ben Loyal, the name a corruption of Ben Laoghal, is often affectionately referred to as the Queen of Scottish Highlands, and with good cause. Not many mountains can be described as beautiful, but Ben Loyal certainly can, compelling admiring attention by its graceful sculpturing and challenging appearance. It takes the form of a long skyline-ridge linking five distinct summits, the whole rising abruptly and in complete isolation from a flat moorland. The effect greatly enhances its stature, although actually its altitude is modest, the highest of its peaks, An Caisteal (the castle) barely topping 2500 feet. The mountain poses perfectly for the camera from the head of the Kyle, where its arresting presence is gloriously displayed.

The ascent is usually started at the farm of Ribigill, south of the village of Tongue, whence shepherds' tracks continue in the direction of the climb. The complete traverse of the mountain is a memorable expedition, made doubly enjoyable by returning the same way. If not climbed, Ben Loyal should at least be seen.

Ben Loyal

After rounding the head of the Kyle, the old road returns north along the west bank to the bridge, there rejoining the A.838 which then aims across country to pass over the River Hope which issues from the freshwater Loch Hope. At this point, another fine mountain, Ben Hope, is revealed as an imposing pyramid in the southern sky.

Looking east towards Ben Hope from Gualin House

BEN HOPE

The name of this splendid mountain appears to be derived from the Norse word *hop*, meaning a bay. Soaring boldly in lonely isolation, Ben Hope conforms to the general conception of a mountain, steep slopes on all sides tapering to a single peak dominating a wide landscape. A minor road skirts its western base but a direct climb from it is ruled out by unremitting steepness and a barrier of rocky buttresses, the ascent usually being made over gentler ground from the north.

Ben Hope has the distinction of being the most northerly Munro in Scotland. A Munro, in climbing parlance, is a Scottish mountain exceeding 3000 feet in height: the name is a tribute to Sir Hugh Munro who, in 1891, published his meticulous records of all the mountains in Scotland over 3000 feet, listing them in descending order of altitude and also arranged in districts, with all the subsidiary tops over 3000 feet but not considered to be separate mountains. Munro's Tables created a challenge enthusiastically taken up by climbers ever since, the ascent of all the 277 Munros being a prime objective of those who find enjoyment in hillwalking. This was an ambition of mine too but a busy working life restricted my activities, and since retirement Anno Domini has done the same, my total bag being no more than a meagre twenty.

It is regrettable that the Ordnance Survey has capitulated to metrication by indicating altitudes in foreign metres on current maps and abandoning good old British feet. I can see no purpose and no sense in this substitution. It seems to me deplorable that proud mountains should be degraded and downgraded thus. Ben Hope's impressive 3040 feet has become a meagre 927 metres to satisfy Brussels and Luxembourg, who couldn't care less. I had hoped that Scottish mountaineers, so proud of their heritage, would say, 'To hell with metres', and remain loyal to the altitudes listed by Munro, but I now find, to my dismay, that the Scottish Mountaineering Club, the publishers of the Tables, in their most recent edition, have also succumbed to Europe and sacrificed a cherished independence by converting all heights to metres. So a Munro is no longer a neat 3000 feet but an untidy 914.4 metres.

Durness is a scattered clifftop community straggling the road, the last outpost of civilisation in the far north, a windswept and cheerless place made tolerable by the welcome and hospitality of hotels and guest houses: it is surprising to find so much accommodation for visitors in so austere an environment. One reason must be that it is the only staging halt within thirty miles; another, more certainly, is the excellence of the seaward views and, in particular, the glorious sweep of the silver sands of Sango Bay and Balnakeil Bay, both exquisitely charming in kind weather. At Balnakeil, reached along a side road, is an establishment of craft workshops.

The greatest single natural attraction of Durness, however, and visited by all who stay or halt there, is the famous Smoo Cave, quickly reached from the road by a much-trodden path leading down to the beach.

SMOO CAVE

The entrance to Smoo Cave is a large opening in the low cliffs bordering the road, the roof being 33 feet above the pebbly beach. There are three chambers in the interior, the outermost, easily accessible, having a length of 200 feet and passing beneath the road, and width of 120 feet. It is a remarkable place, quite the largest sea cave in Scotland, although, oddly, now above the level of high tides. A wet day in Durness need never be completely wasted: Smoo Cave provides shelter, interest and a spice of adventure not found in the hotel lounges.

Smoo Cave

The ferry, Kyle of Durness

The approach to the lighthouse

The A.838 leaves Durness and heads directly for Kylesku and the distant south along the only route permitted by the harsh and uncompromising terrain. It soon comes alongside the Kyle of Durness, yet another sea loch that penetrates far inland. A short side road branches off to a passenger ferry across the Kyle, linking the opposite shore with a narrow strip of tarmac eleven miles long that provides the only access to the lighthouse at Cape Wrath. This journey is a lonely crossing of a desolate, untamed and inhospitable landscape, passing over wild moorlands and a considerable river before reaching its destination. Private cars are not permitted to use the access road and indeed cannot cross via the pedestrian ferry, but in summer months a minibus takes visitors from the ferry to the lighthouse, a service not operating to a timetable and needing to be confirmed by advance enquiry. The ferry too cannot be relied on throughout the year but will generally be available on request. Getting to Cape Wrath is rather chancy.

However, those privileged to make the journey to Cape Wrath can be sure of a memorable experience. Drama erupts when the white tower of the lighthouse finally comes in sight, a thrilling moment, and becomes intense as the vast seascape is viewed from the brink of the cliffs.

Opposite and above *The cliffs of Cape Wrath*

CAPE WRATH

Cape Wrath, the most northerly point of Sutherland, is well named. Nature is in an angry mood here. The Atlantic has waged an unceasing war against this gaunt headland ever since the beginning of time, hurling its waves in fury at the unyielding rocks without respite; there is always the noise of thrashing waters. This is the wildest place in Britain, primitive, raw and undisciplined, with the lighthouse, built in 1848, the only evidence of the intrusion of man. The towering cliffs, rising to a vertical 350 feet below the lighthouse and to 800 feet in places to the east, are the highest in mainland Britain and are virgin, just as they were sculptured, and explored only by the countless seabirds to which they are home. The scenery inspires awe and apprehension and fear even on a summer day; in stormy conditions, the effect is frightening.

Cape Wrath is a good place to visit, but many a genteel tourist will think it a good place to leave.

Strong walkers, and strong walkers only, can follow the coast southwards from Cape Wrath in the hope of arriving in due course at the fishing village of Kinlochbervie. The first seven miles of this journey are extremely arduous: there is no path and progress is a struggle through tussocky grass, tough heather and naked peat hags, keeping to the clifftops where possible but often unavoidably descending into and scrambling out of the coves and gullies that break the ramparts, as well as fording the streams entering the sea from the moorlands of the interior. There are compensations: the cliffs are everywhere impressive, some of the coves are charming, and always there are magnificent views across the North Minch to the island of Lewis in the Outer Hebrides. And always there is the pounding of breakers along the base of the rocks, throwing up white plumes of spray, and always the screaming of the seabirds.

There is a very special reward, however, for those who suffer the rigours of this journey when the cliffs end suddenly to reveal ahead an inviting and welcome crescent of golden sands curving around a lovely bay.

This is Sandwood Bay.

Sandwood Bay

SANDWOOD BAY

Sandwood Bay is a haven of peace in a hostile environment, a jewel in a thorny crown. Its reputation as the most beautiful bay on the west coast of Scotland has developed in recent years, not fostered by press and media publicity but by the enthusiastic recommendations of those who have been there.

It is remote from roads and habitations and can be reached overland only on foot. The easiest and usual route is by a path from near Sheigra, a lonely outpost at the end of the Kinlochbervie road where a sign points the way. Such is the increasing popularity of the bay that the first two miles of the four-mile journey have now been made negotiable for cars, the rest of the journey being on a well-trodden path.

Inland from the bay is Sandwood Loch, its issuing stream crossing the sands to enter the sea.

There are legends attached to Sandwood Bay. Mermaids have been sighted there and a ghost haunts a derelict bothy near the loch. Dreaming the hours away on the lovely sands, one can imagine anything about Sandwood Bay. There is magic in the air.

Where the cliffs resume at the south end of the bay, a remarkable pillar of rock, Am Buachaille (the herdsman) rises vertically from the sea in isolation. This to ordinary mortals seems quite inaccessible but it has been climbed, the first ascent being in 1967.

Am Buachaille

KINLOCHBERVIE HARBOUR

Kinlochbervie is finely situated on a hillside overlooking Loch Inchard, the village being an untidy straggle of buildings bordering the only road which continues for four miles beyond to its terminus at Sheigra. The main interest is centred on the splendid harbour, almost completely landlocked and providing excellent shelter. In recent years, there has been much commercial development here; the facilities have been greatly improved for the fishing vessels and the huge container lorries that transport the catch to the wholesale markets in the cities. There is animated activity on any working day, and Kinlochbervie is now recognised as the most important fishing port in the north-west.

Interestingly, the former harbour, long abandoned, is still to be seen on the other side of the causeway leading to the pier.

The road serving Kinlochbervie is linked to the A.838, branching off at Rhiconich.

Hereabouts the native bedrock of much of Sutherland is evident everywhere on the hillsides and bordering the roads, appearing as outcrops and in patches, pale in colour. This rock is gneiss, and geologists tell us that it is the most ancient of British rocks, extending beyond the mainland to the Hebrides. It gives a strange luminosity to the hills, especially under a dark sky, adding almost a lunar atmosphere to the landscapes. One imagines, probably quite wrongly, that the moon must be like the wilder areas of Sutherland.

Prominent on the eastern horizon are the peaks of Foinaven and Arkle, both names given to racehorses, Foinavon achieving fame as the 1967 Grand National winner and Arkle the triple winner of the Cheltenham Gold Cup. These heights are covered by a capping of quartzite, white in colour and virginal in purity, but splintered and fragmented to such an extent as to make their ascent arduous.

The A.838 leaves Rhiconich, its surface recently improved and widened, to cross colourful foothills to Laxford Bridge.

Kinlochbervie Harbour

Motor roads in Sutherland are few and far between and so are the villages they serve. And distances from one inhabited place to the next are often lengthy, involving hour-long journeys. Filling stations are rarities: it behoves car owners to keep a watch on their reserves of petrol.

The interior of the country is an inhospitable desert of mountains and moors and innumerable lochs: not a desert of desolation but of beautiful and dramatic landscapes. And it is vast: within an area of 2000 square miles, there are no settled communities and very few habitations. The roads are the lifeline of Sutherland: they aim for their destinations as directly as the territory permits, their purposeful progression not deflected by offshoots and alternatives. Road junctions are few and they are of importance to travellers and especially to tourists on a first visit.

Such a junction occurs at Laxford Bridge. It is not marked by a roundabout nor by overhead lighting nor arrows on the tarmac, although modern road signs have replaced the old fingerpost, and indeed the junction is insignificant, merely a meeting of country lanes. A glance at a map, however, shows how vital this junction is. From Durness to Lairg, the centre of communications and supplies, are fifty-seven wilderness miles. In the twenty miles from Durness to Laxford Bridge on the A.838, the only branch is the minor artery to Kinlochbervie and the only roadside building is the hotel at Rhiconich. From Laxford Bridge to Lairg is thirty-seven miles, still on the A.838, and nowhere on this long drive through the Reay Forest and alongside Loch Shin is there a public road branching off until the outskirts of Lairg are reached, and only an occasional shooting lodge or farmstead appears in sight against the background of mountains. Solitude reigns supreme on the A.838.

I have long memories of Lairg. It is no more than a large village with shops, yet to the folk of the remote parts of Sutherland it is a metropolis of great importance. Here the Inverness–Wick railway, which mainly follows the east coast, makes a great loop inland to Lairg Station, this being the nearest point of the line to the coastal villages of the west and north, and here the incoming mail for the whole area is deposited for distribution and the outgoing mail collected for transport on the trains. Roads fan out from Lairg like the open fingers of a hand, each with its separate destination – Lochinver, Scourie, Kinlochbervie, Durness and Tongue – and the postal services along them were undertaken by MacBrayne's buses which left the post offices in these places in the early morning, bringing the day's collection to Lairg for despatch on the railway and returning with the incoming mail from the station. These buses carried supplies and passengers. I was an ardent admirer and supporter of MacBrayne's buses: they opened up the north-west for me. It was a delight to travel on them through exciting scenery that would otherwise have been out of reach.

Many of the roads in the remoter parts of Scotland have been, and are still being, improved and widened, replacing the former single tracks and passing places with fast new roads. Travelling in Sutherland, once hazardous and time-consuming, has become a joy. The roads are very quiet and few cars are met. There are no traffic lights, no pedestrian crossings, no bollards, no tight fences, no traffic wardens, no police traps and, best of all, no yellow lines, single or double. Motorists can shed their chains, stop anywhere and wander off to stretch their legs – not forgetting the camera, a vital piece of equipment in Scotland.

Laxford Bridge is a welcome uninhabited oasis amongst shaggy surroundings. It spans the Laxford River which comes down from a string of lochs alongside the Lairg road and is notable for salmon fishing. There are trees here, inviting a picnic, and a pleasant anglers' path may be followed up-river to bring Ben Stack, the most shapely of the mountains hereabouts, into close view. A little further,

The River Arkle near Laxford Bridge

Arkle is revealed in full stature across the waters of a small loch, a bothy adding a foreground interest to this much-photographed scene. Down-river is the attractive Loch Laxford, an inlet of the sea studded with many small islands.

From Laxford Bridge, the road heading west, the A.894, leads to Scourie but before reaching this village, a narrow side road turns off for Tarbet, a tiny coastal community with a small harbour, normally sleepy and deserted. The presence of a restaurant and public toilets suggests, however, that an influx of visitors is sometimes expected, and such is the case, for across the water and soon reached by boat is the well-known island of Handa.

Handa Island from Tarbet

Opposite *The Great Stack of Handa*   *Badcall Bay*

HANDA ISLAND

Since Handa Island was adopted by the Royal Society for the Protection of Birds in 1962, it has become a mecca for British ornithologists and enthusiastic amateur birdwatchers. The island has the greatest concentration of seabirds in the north-west and at nesting time they are numbered in tens of thousands in a variety of species – guillemot, razorbill, kittiwake, fulmar, puffin, herring gull and shag – creating a deafening cacophony of noise. Falcons, buzzards and golden eagles are sometimes observed but these are occasional visitors.

Sheer cliffs, 300–400 feet high, defend the island, relenting only where a breach permits landings to be made at a small beach; nearby an ancient graveyard and ruined crofts are relics of a former occupation. Today Handa is uninhabited except by birds and is in the care of a warden.

An impressive feature of the cliffs is the Great Stack, a detached pinnacle of sandstone which, incredibly, has been ascended to its flat top by rock-climbers.

Access to the island is permitted and usually made by hired boat from Tarbet across the Sound of Handa; to avoid disappointment, visits should be pre-arranged.

At Scourie, the A.894 reaches the sea and again turns south, now in the close company of a very attractive coastal area, a labyrinth of inlets, bays, cliffs, promontories and lochans in a colourful and confusing array that must have sorely tested the surveyors and cartographers of the Ordnance Survey. A succession of delightful surprises comes into view as the journey proceeds, the gem being Badcall Bay and its seascape of a dozen off-shore islands and, beyond, the vast expanse of Eddrachillis Bay.

The road between Scourie and Kylesku has been changed out of all recognition. It was formerly a narrow single-track with passing places throughout its eleven miles, a slow journey during which the motorist had to keep his foot on the brake and his eyes alert for oncoming cars. Today, however, it is a splendid two-track road, out of character with its surroundings but permitting fast progress – although few will fail to stop often to appraise the changing views around each bend. The scenery is typical Sutherland, with verges of peat, bog myrtle and flag iris, and heathery moors relieved by outcrops of gneiss.

But the biggest changes are reserved for Kylesku.

Quinag across Loch Cairnbawn

KYLESKU

Loch Cairnbawn carries the waters of Eddrachillis Bay deep into the mainland's interior, penetrating the coastal hills, becoming constricted at a narrow strait, and then widening and dividing into Loch Glendhu and Loch Glencoul, both inurned amongst wild mountains. The narrow strait is Kylesku and until recently a car ferry operated across it, this providing the only possible continuation of the main road on the west side of Sutherland. Kylesku was the vital key for travellers to or from the far north, the alternative being a thirty-mile detour to the east. Kylesku was notorious, and approaching cars raced to be in the front of the queue to avoid a frustrating wait. The ferry was free, and funded by the County Council in recognition of their responsibility to ensure an uninterrupted flow of traffic.

Now all is changed. Wide roads lead to a new bridge crossing the water and traffic can proceed at a fast pace without a halt.

Kylesku, to me, is not the same without the ferry. I have waited hours here, usually on the north side, until called forward to the ferry boat and never regretted the delay; anyone with an eye for impressive beauty will not regard time spent at Kylesku as wasted. Twin peaks of Quinag dominate an awe-inspiring picture of great contrasts, of glittering waters cradled in the arms of dark and sinister heights: the silence is profound and the loneliness almost fearful. I could spend a day here, just looking. Kylesku is a wonderful place.

EAS COUL AULIN

Not far from Kylesku but hidden from sight and not easy of access is the highest waterfall in Britain, Eas Coul Aulin, its height being officially stated as 658 feet. A stream of the same name drains a wide moorland above the fall and below it enters the head of Loch Glencoul.

The waterfall may be visited by hiring a boat and boatman (enquire at Kylesku Hotel) for a three-mile voyage to the far end of this loch, whence a short walk brings it into view.

It may be reached on foot by using a track leaving the Ullapool road four miles out of Kylesku: this climbs over a high saddle before reaching the stream which can be followed down to the lip of the fall. The steep east bank may be descended, with care, for a more comprehensive view. The return must be made along the same track: a rough walk, there and back, of six miles.

Eas Coul Aulin

Below *Loch Glendhu and Loch Glencoul*

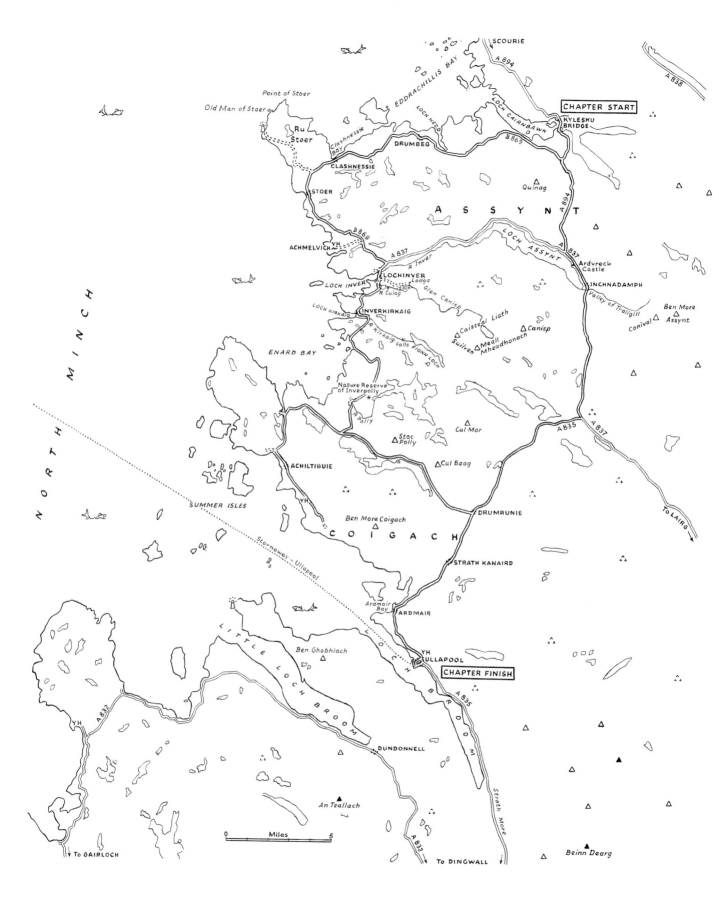

ASSYNT AND COIGACH

THERE HAVE also been changes at the south end of the Kylesku Bridge, where the little cluster of buildings where vehicles formerly embarked on the ferry boat is now bypassed by the new road. Gone is the apprehension and excitement of the approach, and gone too is the romance. The primitive inn that catered for travellers who had missed the last ferry is now a modern hotel, and commercial interests have been attracted by the growing number of tourists.

The district now entered on the journey south is Assynt. A road, still the A.894, leaves Kylesku, climbs to a low pass with the huge mass of Quinag on the right and declines to the shore of Loch Assynt, where it joins the A.837 from Lochinver near the sad lochside ruin of Ardvreck Castle. A little further on is Inchnadamph. Here, reached only by walking, is the lovely valley of Traligill, a place of alpine flowers and limestone caves and formations, backed by the intimidating peaks of Conival and Ben More Assynt. The road goes on, in spectacular scenery, to Ullapool, thirty-four miles from Kylesku, a journey now easily accomplished in an hour but which took half a day before the roads were widened and improved to their present high standard.

The best of Assynt, however, lies between this road and the coast, and my preference is always to turn off the A.894 two miles out of Kylesku and go along a narrow road that has never been improved and I hope never will. Although having a B classification, it is little better than a country lane, yet, despite some sudden halts and reversings and generally slow progress, is a delight to follow. Time doesn't matter in surroundings of such loveliness. Initially the road winds through woodlands of birch and alder and hazel and oak uncharacteristic of the harsh Sutherland terrain and alongside a dancing beck; it then crosses an open moor between the buttresses of Quinag and the waters of Loch Cairnbawn.

It is a switchback journey with many ups and downs and one particularly steep descent almost to sea level where Loch Nedd bites deeply into the coastline. Here too there are trees in profusion, and although habitations are sparse, there is no feeling of loneliness; indeed, when the few buildings of Drumbeg are reached, there is hospitality on offer. The hotel here is a well-known resort of anglers who have a choice of a dozen nearby lochs and lochans for their sport. On goes the road in a series of turns and twists and interesting situations, with intriguing glimpses of the coast and the wide sweep of Eddrachillis Bay, and then the vast seascape is fully revealed as the road comes alongside the lovely Clashnessie Bay, bounded and sheltered in the west by a peninsula that thrusts far out to sea and ends at the rocky Point of Stoer.

Clashnessie Bay

As the road leaves Clashnessie Bay, the hamlet of the same name is passed and after a further mile a side road turns off to the right and crosses the bare and windswept peninsula, the Ru Stoer, to a lighthouse where it ends at a parking place for cars. Rather unexpectedly, the lighthouse is not situated at the far extremity of the headland, the Point of Stoer, but two miles short on the west side. It is an exhilarating walk to the Point, where the cliffs tower to a height of 300 feet, but the great feature that tempts motorists from their cars is a spectacular detached column of rock that rises 200 feet out of the angry waves at its base. This is the Old Man of Stoer and incredibly has been climbed to its top, the first time in 1966.

The Old Man of Stoer

Stoer Lighthouse

After this recommended detour to Ru Stoer, the road to Lochinver is resumed as it turns south and passes between the scattered buildings of the village of Stoer, occupying a bleak area of the coastal belt and itself having no features of special interest to warrant a halt, but blessed with a lovely bay and sandy beaches nearby. Then as the journey proceeds the harshness of the Stoer landscape softens, the road winding amongst low heathery hills and skirting the shores of many small lochans. The next few miles are delectable and not to be hurried, and indeed are better appreciated by a traveller on foot than in a car. Every turn of the road brings fresh and intimate vistas of unspoilt charm. Here beauty is not formally arranged: Nature has been haphazard and untidy, scattering boulders and trees and outcropping rocks and peat mosses in bewitching confusion amid the colourful tapestries of the enclosing heights. Loveliness is lavishly displayed.

A side road turns off to Achmelvich, renowned for its rocky coast and excellent sandy beaches, but on a recent visit I was disappointed to find the place robbed of its appeal by a tight concentration of caravans. Goodbye, Achmelvich.

Finally, the road joins the main highway into Lochinver, the A.837 from Ullapool, and in a short mile the main street is entered.

LOCHINVER

When I was first studying the map of Scotland and planning itineraries, Lochinver was a magic name, and has remained so. In those early days, its isolation on the distant north-west coast seemed to make it unattainable by anyone who had only feet to get him there and whose opportunities were restricted by a busy working life south of the Border, although later I was to discover that a MacBrayne's bus made the forty-six-mile journey to and from Lairg every weekday. Lochinver was a magnet, largely because of the strange mountains I knew to be in its vicinity, and I longed to go there. My first visit was accomplished by walking, an experience I shall recount later.

Lochinver fully lives up to expectations. It is a curving half-mile of cottages and assorted buildings lining a single street and facing a loch that has carved a channel inland from the open sea and given the village its name. An island at the mouth of the loch and a wooded hill provide shelter for the splendid harbour, the home of a fleet of fishing boats. Hotels and guest houses and cafés cater for the summer influx of visitors.

The charms of Lochinver are not found in the village, however, but in the immediate environs and in the hinterland. Two rivers enter the loch: the River Inver, coming down amongst trees from the hills behind, has a pleasant path alongside much used by anglers, with fishing platforms built over the rushing waters. The other river is the Culag, which descends a rocky channel in a succession of white cataracts, a spectacular sight in times of spate.

It is the hinterland that has the greatest appeal. From a wilderness of heathery undulations and turbulent streams, peaty quagmires and innumerable inland lochs in this strangest of Scottish landscapes, there rise the mountains of west Assynt, springing up suddenly and steeply and assuming weird and fantastic shapes. The greatest of these is Suilven.

Lochinver village from the harbour

Above right and left *The Rivers Inver and Culag*

Opposite *Suilven*

SUILVEN

Suilven is not easy to believe. Its grotesque outline keeps popping into view unexpectedly wherever one walks or drives around Lochinver, appearing as a giant thimble and always seeming to be peering inquisitively to see what is happening. A sudden sight of it is startling. It arrests attention.

The mountain is seen from the west as a massive dome ringed by cliffs; from the east, it takes the shape of a slender pinnacle. In fact, these are the two extremities of a mile-long ridge. The dome seen from Lochinver is Caisteal Liath, the highest summit; the sharp peak seen from the east is Meall Mheadhonach. They are linked by a narrow ridge which dips in the middle to a saddle. Purists recognise a third peak, Meall Bheag, divided from the east peak by a deep cleft, but this is relatively insignificant.

The ascent of Suilven is the grandest expedition available from Lochinver and is a challenge to both mountaineers and experienced hillwalkers for whom there are only two possible routes of ascent, one on the north flank and the other on the south. The most direct approach leaves the village by way of Glen Canisp, taking advantage of a rough road to a shooting lodge and then continuing on a good track along the north base of the mountain until opposite the obvious saddle; here the track, which heads for the more orthodox mountain of Canisp, is left and a watery beeline made for the foot of the gully descending from the saddle. The gully is steep and rough but not beyond the ability of an average walker, and leads unerringly to the depression on the ridge, whence a simple climb up to the right leads to the summit cairn of Caisteal Liath. The view is stunning, a prospect of water rather than land, with lochs in profusion and the sea beyond; and strange isolated peaks fill the landward horizon. But the most arresting feature is the amazing spire of Meall Mheadhonach at the other end of the ridge.

Suilven, from the River Kirkaig

No direct descent from the summit of Caisteal Liath is possible other than by falling off it to a certain death, and steps must be retraced to the saddle, where another gully, a counterpart to that used in the ascent, offers an alternative route of return to Lochinver. This descends the south flank and is initially rough, but reaches a clear path that winds round Fionn Loch and leads down in surroundings that become idyllic. The path is accompanied by the River Kirkaig, which has a fine waterfall, to Inverkirkaig, three miles from Lochinver by road.

This alternative route of return is strongly recommended. The round trip of some twelve miles is one of the finest of mountain expeditions.

The River Kirkaig

The only motor road out of Lochinver, other than the A.837, leaves the village near the harbour and ascends alongside the River Culag to the loch from which it issues. Here, on a little promontory, is the village school, surely the most beautifully situated building in Britain for learning the three Rs. Suilven is in view across the loch, its bizarre outline holding the gaze as the road continues in very pretty surroundings by the water's edge, soon climbing and crossing more open country with glorious views of the rocky coast before descending to the shore of Loch Kirkaig and the little community of Inverkirkaig.

Inverkirkaig

The road by Enard Bay

THE MAD LITTLE ROAD OF SUTHERLAND

So called although prior to the reorganisation of local government boundaries in 1974, the road was almost wholly within the neighbouring county of Ross and Cromarty. No matter. Now absorbed in the new Highland Region, it is still there and as mad as ever.

This road is my favourite in all Scotland. It is an utter delight all the way, especially for travellers on foot with time to linger, but perhaps not for nervous motorists. It leaves Inverkirkaig by a pleasant avenue alongside the River Kirkaig, formerly the county boundary, and reaches a bridge across it. Here we say farewell to Sutherland.

The road, a single car's width, now heads south on a tortuous journey of ups and downs and ins and outs through a tangled landscape of low hillocks, gneiss outcrops, peat bogs and small lochans that lap the roadside verges, furnished with occasional clumps of trees and bordered by heather and gorse: an undisciplined maze yet endowed with infinite beauty. Surprises are around every corner. The narrow strip of tarmac, not enclosed by fences, winds free in a continuous search for easy passage. In places, it escapes from confining boulder slopes and low cliffs and gives uninterrupted views across a wild moorland interspersed with sheets of water to the distant mountains soaring abruptly skywards in complete isolation as though not on speaking terms with each other. For mile after mile, the road threads a way forward, sometimes turning inland to avoid the rocky shore, sometimes hugging the coast to avoid the impenetrable inland. When it comes alongside Enard Bay, where seals may be seen, the scenery is exquisite, out of this world.

In due course, and all too soon, the excitement of the scenery fades as the road declines through woodland to the only buildings, the Nature Reserve of Inverpolly, there crossing the River Polly and climbing over a bare moorland dominated by Stac Polly, here seen end on as a slender spire, and then finally joins the Ullapool–Achiltibuie road.

On my first acquaintance with the mad little road, in about 1950, I had no feelings of affection for it nor any eye for the beauty all around, my gaze being fixed on the tarmac ahead as I dragged weary legs along it.

I had arrived at Ullapool by bus in mid-afternoon, determined to satisfy an ambition to make a first visit to Lochinver. I planned an overnight stay at the Drumrunie Hotel, marked on the map and ten miles along the road, but when I tried to telephone to book a room, the operator told me that the hotel had recently been burnt down. Nevertheless I set off northwards, feeling sure that there would be other accommodation along the way. As I rounded Ardmair Bay, the sky was bright but as I reached the scattered cottages and crofts of Strath Kanaird, none with an invitation to halt or stop, ominous yellow clouds formed overhead, obviously heralding a storm, and when Stac Polly came into sight, there was a spiralling column like a tornado above it. The sky was evil and frightening. It was early evening in May but already darkness was closing over the landscape. The rain came as I reached the drive of the hotel, set amongst trees, and I ventured along it in search of shelter.

The hotel was a shell, the roof having collapsed completely, but a few yards of the verandah ceiling remained intact and under it I spent the most wretched night of my life, standing in a dry corner, listening to the drenching rain and howling wind and breathing in the acrid fumes of the recent fire. The night became bitterly cold. I stamped around my little island of dry ground to keep warm, chain-smoking, but long before midnight I was shivering uncontrollably. I pulled on my pyjamas over my other clothes, but without any beneficial effect . . . My vigil lasted eight miserable hours until, mercifully, in the grey light of dawn, the downpour ceased. Off I went, thankful to stretch my legs again, but ravenously hungry, not having eaten since breakfast the day before.

I kept to my itinerary, turning off along the Achiltibuie road, passing below the serrated skyline of Stac Polly, its upper rocks tinged pink as the sun rose over the horizon. When at last I came to the start of the mad little road to Lochinver, I followed it over the bleak moorland, Stac Polly now appearing as a black spire in a halo of sunlight. I came down to Inverpolly, then a farm, but there was no sign of life. I was near exhaustion as I slowly toiled up the incline beyond. Hours went by as I dragged my legs over the next few miles. I walked as in a nightmare, aware of nothing but the few yards of tarmac ahead and stopping every few yards. The sun became relentlessly hot, adding dehydration to my distress; I stripped off my pyjamas and restored them to the rucksack. I was famished, having had no food or sleep for thirty hours. To cap all I suffered a physical hallucination as I staggered up the road beyond the inlet of Enard Bay: I could clearly see a row of cottages at the top of the hill but when I got there, they had vanished. I was, if you will pardon the expression, absolutely buggered.

By mid-afternoon I finally reached Inverkirkaig, not having seen anybody nor been passed by a car since leaving Ullapool. I tottered across to a cottage on the edge of the loch and asked for a pot of tea and a bite to eat. The residents, a kind couple, took compassion on me and provided my needs, refusing payment. After this, I felt a little refreshed but as I came over the hill towards Lochinver, my legs rebelled. I could walk no further. A nearby cottage displayed a B and B sign; I swayed across to it, was admitted by an elderly lady and collapsed in a chair. I begged a meal. The lady settled me comfortably and then left the cottage. I sank into a stupor. Two hours later she returned, busied herself in the kitchen and then produced a huge plate loaded with fish and potatoes, and a mammoth pot of tea. I wolfed the lot and crawled upstairs to bed, requesting an early call so that I could catch the 8.30 bus from Lochinver, still nearly three miles further on, to Lairg.

Bless the lady: she gave me a large breakfast and then told me she had arranged with a friend who had a car to take me into Lochinver. So I reached Lochinver in style, had time to look around, and mounted the bus outside the post office: the morning's collection of mail and I were the only passengers.

There was a sequel to this adventure. An office colleague to whom I had told my story, went to Lochinver by train and bus a few months later and stayed at the same cottage. The lady remembered my visit well, said she had been concerned about me and confided that, to provide me with a good meal, she had walked the five miles into Lochinver and back to buy fresh fish.

This was an example of Highland hospitality I was to find repeated often. Before visiting the remote north, I had rather expected the folk there to be rough, uncouth, possibly even hostile. I was totally wrong. Wherever I went, I found them gentle, quietly spoken, very kind and anxious to be helpful. Visitors might be abrasive at times but never the natives. Over nearly fifty years, I have developed a great affection for them. They are my favourite people.

ACHILTIBUIE

Achiltibuie in Coigach is literally out on a limb. Every time I go, I feel I am approaching the end of the world.

Going south from Lochinver, the road reaches a T-junction, left to Ullapool, but a diversion to the right, to Achiltibuie, is recommended. This road crosses a bare headland, leaving behind all the exciting scenery, and seven miles further on curves round to the coast and enters the village of Achiltibuie, continuing beyond past other smaller communities until brought to a stop by the steep slopes of Ben More Coigach, the huge mountain dominating both land and sea hereabouts. The village and coastline have an air of sadness because of the many ruined crofts facing the water, but there is hospitality for the many visitors.

The charm of Achiltibuie lies in the seaward prospect to a group of islands, the Summer Isles, and especially across the wide breadth of Loch Broom to the lofty heights beyond Dundonnell and Gair-loch. Achiltibuie is at its best on a fine sunny day of clear visibility.

Returning to the T-junction, the road to Ullapool is followed along the side of Stac Polly.

Loch Broom from Achiltibuie

Stac Polly

STAC POLLY

Stac Polly is an extraordinary mountain when seen from a distance and doubly so when one is engaged on the traverse of its narrow ridge. It is a dwarf among the fellow heights of Assynt and Coigach, having an altitude of 2009 feet only, but its ascent presents difficulties far greater than those of many a Munro.

It rises starkly from steep slopes topped by crags and its striking appearance is emphasised by detached isolation. Soaring like a sharp wedge, its sandstone rocks have defied the storms of ages but have been split and shattered into a succession of strange pinnacles requiring the skill of rockclimbers to surmount although, by trial and error, walkers can make progress by avoiding the crest of the ridge in places of difficulty, using stony gullies for descent and re-ascent. This is an exercise leading to sensational but safe situations and ultimately, with care, to the summit cairn at the west end of the mountain. As on Suilven, the ridge dips to an easy saddle and rises to an east top.

The views are magnificent: of extensive sheets of water backed by imposing heights, Cul Beag and Cul Mor filling the eastern sky and the sprawling mass of Ben More Coigach across a deep trench to the south, every prospect enhanced by the spectacular array of pinnacles in the foreground, subjects for a score of camera studies.

Stac Polly is a popular challenge. A large roadside car park has been made and from it a track has been worn to the saddle on the ridge; the steep climb has been helped by this path formed since my first visit. The drama starts when the skyline is reached.

Professor Heddle referred to Stac Polly as 'a porcupine in a state of extreme irascibility'. There could not be a more apt description of this mountain in miniature.

Cul Mor, from Stac Polly   Below *Ben More Coigach, from Stac Polly*

Cul Beag

From the Stac Polly car park, the road continues eastwards through scenes of mountain grandeur, skirting the lower slopes of Cul Beag and reaching the main road, now the A.835, coming from Kylesku or Lairg and heading south to Ullapool, with retrospective views of Stac Polly until declining into Strath Kanaird and arriving on the coast at Ardmair Bay.

There is a lovely panorama of the bay as the road climbs beyond, the curve of the golden sands, the open expanse of sea and the massive bulk of Ben More Coigach in the background combining in a picture of surpassing beauty. But alas, it was destroyed when I was there recently by a long line of caravans along the beach. A few decades of road improvements have encouraged motorists to visit beauty spots formerly difficult of access. Cars and caravans always mar a scene.

The road tops a hill and commences a long descent to a built-up area that, even when seen at a distance, is obviously a place of greater importance than any yet seen on the journey. It is Ullapool.

Ardmair Bay

ULLAPOOL

Ullapool is a large village with pretensions to the status of a small town. Certainly, although having a resident population of just over a thousand, it can claim to be the capital of a very extensive area of the north, there being no larger town within forty miles. There are shops in plenty, banks, hotels, guest houses and many private houses within a pattern of streets apparently not developed haphazardly, but laid to a master plan. Such is the case: Ullapool was designed by a Fisheries Association in 1788 as a base for the herring industry and today the centre of activity is still the splendid harbour, a place of boats and bustle and screaming seagulls. It increased in importance latterly when Ullapool took over from Kyle of Lochalsh as the port of departure and arrival of the Stornoway ferry.

I first visited Ullapool just after the war. I had noticed the name on a map but had never read a mention of it so went there in some trepidation: it seemed remote, so far from towns and railways. I was alone, on foot, and hardly knew what to expect. I was surprised to find there an air of prosperity and sophistication, large hotels catering for tourists, much activity at the harbour and more people on the streets than I thought there would be. . . . Since then, Ullapool has flourished exceedingly, having become extremely popular as a holiday resort, its seasonal visitors further augmented by those using the Stornoway boat. At peak periods, the streets are crowded.

The attractions of Ullapool are not altogether in its intrinsic interests. A beautiful situation on lovely Loch Broom, facing west to the opposite shore and the sheltering height of Ben Ghobhlach, a good road bringing the wonders of Assynt and Sutherland within easy reach by car, and the picturesque environs of the loch and the lush valley at its head, Strath More – all these contribute to the popular appeal.

Ullapool today is too busy for my liking, but simply must be included in the itineraries of those in search of the best of northern Scotland.

Ullapool, from the harbour   Opposite *Loch Broom*

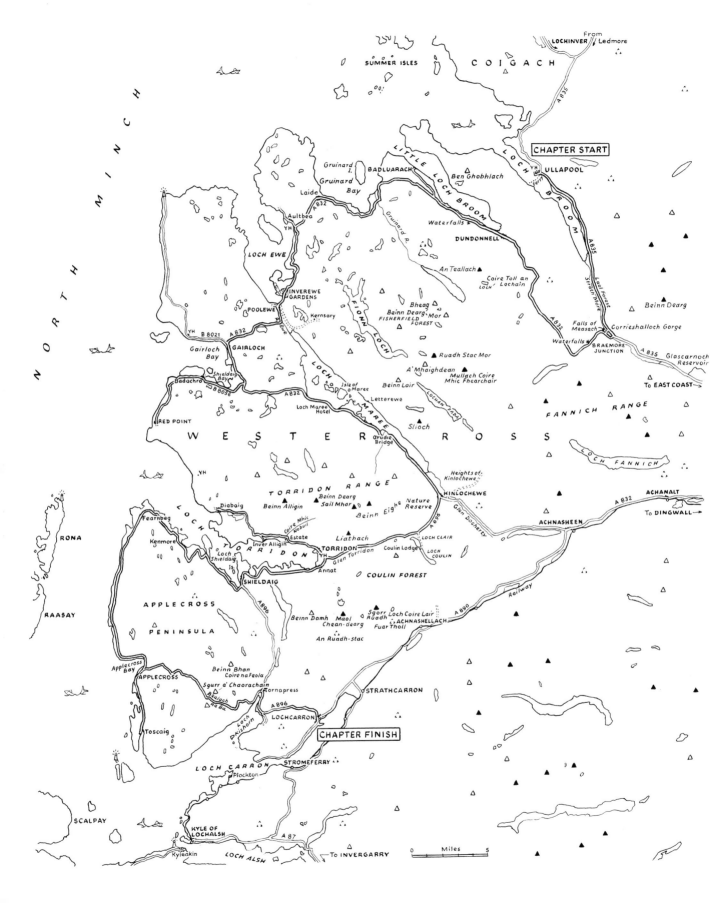

WESTER ROSS

I F I HAD been writing this chapter twenty years ago, I would have headed it Wester Ross or Ross-shire without hesitation, and still prefer to do so despite the absorption of the area into the new county of Highland Region in 1974. To me and thousands more the name of Wester Ross lives on. We were brought up to think of the wonderland between Loch Broom and the roads to Skye as Wester Ross, and always will.

There are two ways from Ullapool for southbound travellers. Walkers in a hurry can sneak across on a passenger ferry and over the facing hill on a cart track to Dundonnell, saving nearly twenty miles and the best part of a day. But motorists, explorers and connoisseurs of beauty will follow the usual route departing along the A.835. They will be amply rewarded. . . . After two miles, a halt should be made to look back at Ullapool, a lovely picture with the odd effect that the buildings seem to be floating on the waters of Loch Broom.

Ullapool

The road goes on amid scenery of increasing charm along the bonny banks of the loch, which at its head is succeeded by the emerald pastures and rich woodlands of Strath More. The trees here, of all varieties and including rhododendrons, are a delight, the road being turned into a gracious avenue by noble specimens. Rising on the left are the extensive plantations of Lael Forest. The valley narrows as the enclosing heights crowd in and the road ascends to a large car park and signs inviting a visit to the Falls of Measach nearby. Admission is free, sightseeing passers-by crossing the road to the entrance where a short path leads down amongst trees to a viewing platform.

CORRIESHALLOCH GORGE

The viewing platform for the Falls of Measach is sensationally poised above a tremendous chasm, the waterfalls and a rushing river being seen in the gloomy depths far below. This fearful cleft, a mile long and hundreds of feet deep, is Corrieshalloch Gorge, a natural wonder, a spectacle unique and, at first sight, startling and even alarming. Vertical cliffs overhung by trees plunge down to a tumult of waters in a sunless channel, a scene of evil portent, a black pit in total contrast to the bright woodland above and along the fringes of the gulf, the summer foliage partly obstructing the downward view – to the despair of enthusiastic photographers.

A much-trodden path also threads a way up-river through the trees, keeping clear of the precipitous edge, to a bridge spanning the gorge, this too revealing a frightening prospect far beneath. Corrieshalloch Gorge is not for the timid and sufferers from nightmares but it must be seen. There is no other place like it.

Resuming the journey, a most important meeting of roads is soon reached at Braemore Junction. The A.835 goes straight forward, crossing the watershed of the Highlands and ultimately arriving at the east coast. Turning off is the A.832 bound for Gairloch, forty-five miles distant on the west coast. Should the junction be overlooked in darkness or mist, an error is irretrievable without returning, these being the only two motor roads in a wide area. Mammoth road signs do their best to ensure that such oversights do not occur.

At Braemore, we are again in the close company of giants. To the north, hidden by foothills and in a remote deer forest, is a complex of Munros grouped around Beinn Dearg, at 3547 feet the

Corrieshalloch Gorge from the Falls of Measach

Glascarnoch Reservoir

highest mountain in Scotland north of the A.835. This group is splendidly seen either by walking up through Lael Forest to the bare heights above or, without effort and indeed without leaving the car by proceeding six miles further along the A.835 from Braemore to Glascarnoch Reservoir, where the highest peaks are well displayed.

Leaving Braemore by the A.832, the long circuit of the Gairloch peninsula commences. It is a devious route around the coastal fringes, no direct way across the intervening wilderness of mountains being possible except on foot by strong walkers.

Almost immediately there is a beautiful retrospect of Loch Broom and Strath More; seen under a blue sky, there are few fairer pictures than this.

Further along, after passing roadside waterfalls, the high ground on the left takes impressive shape as the western peaks of the Fannich range come into view.

Loch Broom, from the A.832

THE FANNICHS

Occupying a tract of wild country between the only two roads linking west and east in Ross-shire, the Fannich range is a formidable barrier of high peaks extending for ten miles and separated by low passes from other mountain areas. A complete traverse of the range includes the ascent of nine summits exceeding 3000 feet in altitude and the Fannichs are therefore a magnet for Munro-baggers. Less active mountain enthusiasts whose preference is merely to capture Munros with a camera may do so by climbing the ridge north of the Achnasheen–Achanalt road and railway. From the crest of this ridge, a comprehensive view of the range unfolds: a magnificent panorama especially when the tops are under snow, the long array of peaks being seen across the deep trench of Loch Fannich which forms the southern boundary of the group over a distance of eight miles.

I was once on the ridge with my wife, taking photographs, when the silence was shattered suddenly by the scream of a low-flying jet aeroplane; in a matter of seconds, it skimmed over the full length of the loch, rose a little in the upper valley and then appeared to turn sharply into the mountain wall, passing from sight and sound. We were convinced we had witnessed a terrible accident and hurried to the police station at Lochcarron to report the incident, there to be reassured that there had not been a crash, and gently rebuked for assuming there had been. Incidents such as this are often reported without foundation, we were told. Curious, I later studied a large-scale map of the Fannichs, and sure enough there was a narrow-sided glen where the aeroplane had vanished: the pilot must have turned into it, risen over the col at the head and continued his flight northwards. I pass on the advice given by the Lochcarron police: Don't panic, the pilots know what they are doing and where they are going.

The western Fannichs

Destitution Road

The Fannichs are left behind as the road from Braemore turns north-west and enters a wide and barren landscape for several miles. This section of the road, formerly narrow and dusty, was known as the Destitution Road, made in the middle of the last century to relieve unemployment and poverty – and road improvements have not lessened the loneliness of the journey. Once there was a wayside inn, now a pathetic ruin. But there is one redeeming feature: directly ahead and growing in stature with every stride or turn of the wheels, is the serrated and exciting skyline of An Teallach, a mountain supreme.

When An Teallach passes from sight behind foothills, the road turns down to scenery of a very different character, to the beautiful trees and parklands of Dundonnell and vistas of sylvan charm. An Teallach reappears at close range and dominates the scene, refusing to be ignored.

An Teallach, from the woods of Dundonnell

AN TEALLACH

It would be an exaggeration to say that An Teallach is to Dundonnell as the Matterhorn is to Zermatt, yet mountaineers do come to Dundonnell because of An Teallach. The full traverse of its dizzy crest is best left to the experts, but all active visitors should at least make an effort to see its magnificent eastern corrie, Coire Toll an Lochain, the showpiece of the mountain. A visit is possible by using either one of two tracks. The most obvious is a cart track leaving the road when it declines to valley level: this leads uphill amongst trees to a vast plateau but passes a boggy mile distant from the corrie. This track, incidentally, is the start or finish of the greatest of all wilderness walks in Scotland (*see* p. 55). The other track is to be preferred, leading directly to the corrie and the most exciting aspect of the mountain, but the way is very rough and not for feet in sandals. It leaves the road nearer the Dundonnell Hotel, where the stream issuing from the corrie passes beneath, and climbs in close company to bouldery ground above the dark waters of Loch Toll an Lochain with the cliffs of An Teallach towering immediately beyond in an intimidating wall of crags and scree. This scene, in my opinion, is the most impressive example of mountain architecture in the country, overwhelming in its majesty. The effect is overpowering, intimidating. Legs turn to jelly at the thought of scaling those awful precipices; mine do, anyway. This awesome aspect of An Teallach is a highlight never forgotten and well repays the five miles of rough walking before regaining the smooth road.

Beyond the Dundonnell Hotel, the road comes alongside the headwaters of Little Loch Broom which penetrates far inland on a course parallel with its bigger twin, the peninsula of Ben Ghobhlach dividing the two. The next few miles following the shoreline seem tame after the excitement of An Teallach and most interest is centred on the expanding views seawards, the only intimate feature of note being a very pretty wayside waterfall. There are signs of civilisation along here, with a scattering of crofts and farmsteads, and a narrow road branches off to the isolated community of Badluarach, a lonely outpost at the entrance to Little Loch Broom.

The A.832 continues forward, rising as it crosses a bare and uninteresting moorland, any feeling of desolation being relieved by the sight of the Summer Isles and Coigach across the open sea. At the top of the rise, in rougher terrain, the scenery improves dramatically as Gruinard Bay is suddenly revealed ahead.

Opposite *A wayside waterfall*
Loch Toll an Lochain

GRUINARD BAY

Gruinard Bay is a renowned beauty spot with an element of surprise. Here are houses of distinction and cottages of charm favoured by lovely trees and gardens, an oasis of greenery in marked contrast to the savage background of rugged heights from which the Gruinard River rushes through a gorge. The bay itself is extensive, four miles either way, with a rocky coastline of coves and beaches of sand and shingle. Gruinard Island is prominent off-shore: this was commandeered by the military authorities during the last war for experiments in chemical weapons, the ground being so contaminated that approaches to it were forbidden for forty years afterwards, the ban only recently being lifted.

The road climbs steeply from the bay to a popular viewpoint at a bad corner often congested by parked cars, causing a traffic hazard that the road engineers have made repeated efforts to remedy, their task being made difficult by a rocky cutting through which the road passes.

Gruinard Bay

Loch Ewe

After leaving Gruinard Bay, the landscape is again rather dreary, lacking trees, as the road follows the coast to Laide where it turns south and crosses a headland to Aultbea and Loch Ewe. Hereabouts, there are more signs of human occupation, albeit still on a small scale: small townships, scattered crofts, and a few large hotels to suggest that we are entering an area frequented by tourists. The surroundings, however, are bleak, and interest is confined to the wide expanse of Loch Ewe, an inlet of the sea of considerable extent, commissioned into service during the war as a base to assist in the passage of convoys, when there was a submarine boom across the entrance. There is still a naval establishment at the water's edge, the road passing above it and sweeping around a hillside towards a distant prospect of great promise.

The road gradually descends into kinder surroundings, the sight of trees being welcome after the barren crossing from Gruinard, and arrives at a car park as large as a football field, usually well patronised by cars and coaches and obviously indicating the presence of a major attraction.

Adjacent are the most famous gardens in Scotland.

INVEREWE GARDENS

The romantic story of the creation of the wonderful gardens at Inverewe has often been told and they have been pictured frequently on television. In the middle of the last century, a local landowner of rare imagination, Osgood Mackenzie, conceived the idea of transforming a barren and rocky promontory of Loch Ewe into a wild garden in which, blessed by the influence of the Gulf Stream, trees and shrubs would be persuaded to flourish in defiance of the harsh northern climate. It was a challenge he tackled with unabated energy over many years, helped by his estate workers. First a sturdy windbreak of native pines was planted to provide shelter, the land was drained, the boggy ground reclaimed, rock crevices filled in and paths made. In the course of a long lifetime, his bold concept was proved an amazing success. Trees and shrubs and plants from all parts of the world were introduced and encouraged to feel at home; Inverewe became tropical. After his death, the good work was continued by his daughter who, in 1952, gave the property to the National Trust for Scotland. In their care, the gardens have continued to be maintained excellently but rather as a commercial undertaking: there are innovations in the form of an expensive gift shop and tea-room – developments of which I doubt Osgood would have approved. He planted for pleasure, not profit.

Inverewe House   Opposite *Inverewe Gardens*

Poolewe Bridge

Beyond Inverewe is Poolewe, a picturesque village overlooking the head of Loch Ewe at the point where the rushing River Ewe enters the loch. Here seals may be seen bobbing in the calm waters. The village stands at the terminus of the great trench occupied by the inland Loch Maree, the river forming a link.

Visitors are catered for by hotels, guest houses and a large caravan park and many of them have a regular clientele.

Poolewe, too, offers an opportunity to take a peep into an area often described as 'the last great wilderness of Scotland'.

THE LAST GREAT WILDERNESS

The rugged mountain region between Little Loch Broom and Loch Maree is regarded with affection and apprehension by conservationists and mountaineers alike, their concern being to keep it as an unspoilt wilderness against the growing threat of infiltration by unsympathetic tourists and insensitive planners. The reason for this jealous safeguarding of a natural heritage is apparent to, and surely supported by, all who know the area. This is indeed a precious landscape, a region remote from the influence of man: 300 square miles in extent with one habitation only. The place appears exactly as it has done through the ages, the only signs of man's intrusion being a ruined bothy, an insecure foot-bridge and the thin track worn by hardy walkers. Quite hidden from the solitary road around the perimeter, the A.832, the interior can be reached only on foot and the mountains climbed only by the toughest of adventurers. Here is nature at its most raw, manifest in savage peaks and towering preci-pices, in awesome acres of naked rock and bogs, in lonely lochs and silent glens. The pattern is con-fusing, yet fascinating; a good map is an essential companion for anyone daring to penetrate this wildest of sanctuaries. The loneliness is acute, the silence absolute.

Of the mountains, An Teallach is the finest and can be seen from the road at Dundonnell, and Slioch is a familiar object overlooking Loch Maree in the south, but those in the inner fastnesses are out of sight or imperfectly glimpsed. Beinn Lair, A' Mhaighdean, the twins Beinn Dearg Mor and Bheag, Mullach Coire Mhic Fhearchair and Ruadh Stac Mor, the latter recently promoted to Munro status – all these are mountains with magic and mystery in their stones and are unknown but to a few. Lochan Fada, Fionn Loch and a score of other water expanses, jewels in sunlight, sullen under cloud, are rarely seen. There is a brooding quiet over everything, a perfect antidote to urban clamour.

Poolewe and Dundonnell are at the ends of a classic walk of nearly thirty miles crossing this wilder-ness and, because of the rigours of the journey, calling for careful advance planning. There is a track, good in places but often intermittent. It is an expedition only for the very fit: weaklings and novices must expect to perish. Once committed, there is no easy escape.

However, all the hidden peaks and lochs can be seen satisfactorily by three shorter forays to the verge of the interior, suitable for the moderately fit.

From Poolewe, a private road may be followed to the isolated croft of Kernsary (cars may be taken thus far with permission), whence a track used by anglers leads up to Fionn Loch; from it, branches

the wilderness route to Dundonnell, entering a vast basin with an exciting array of mountains ahead, Beinn Lair and A' Mhaighdean being prominent. The track can be followed easily for some miles before returning.

From Dundonnell a cart track leads up from the road to the plateau of An Teallach and can be followed until the twin peaks of Beinn Dearg come into sight.

From Kinlochewe there is a third route, to be described when we get there.

Beinn Lair

A' Mhaighdean

Below *Beinn Dearg Mor and Beinn Dearg Bheag*

A distant glimpse of Loch Maree

From Poolewe, a narrow road follows the coast to the headland west of Loch Ewe but is of interest only to the few residents alongside it, and visitors invariably continue on the A.832 to Gairloch, this road also having been brought up to modern standards. It climbs up to and over a ridge and on the ascent reveals an exquisite vista of Loch Maree, a foretaste of joys to come.

As the ridge is topped, new scenes unfold ahead. Gairloch Bay comes into sight with the open waters of the North Minch beyond, as the road descends to the village beautifully situated along the shore.

GAIRLOCH

Gairloch has long been renowned as a holiday resort of rare distinction, Victorian visitors regularly patronising the large hotel overlooking the bay and enjoying the quiet seclusion of this favoured backwater. Nowadays, it is rather more garish, a popular halt for coaches, but nothing can detract from the superb views over the rocky coast and lovely sands, the road serving as a promenade. The village faces west to a distant horizon formed by Skye and the Torridon mountains, a glorious prospect. The older part at the south end has a small harbour and pier and is especially charming, mature woodlands creating an Arcadia of delight.

Gairloch Bay

A no-through-road follows the coast of the northern headland of Gairloch for several miles, supplying small townships and crofts along the way. The A.832 now heads south up a wooded ravine, rising pleasantly to open country, the latter section of the climb being defaced by a huge water pipe coming down from a reservoir above: a black mark for the planners and water authorities. Above the trees, a road branches off to Badachro and Red Point.

RED POINT

A detour to Red Point is worth making only in conditions of exceptionally clear visibility; in dull or misty weather, it is a fruitless exercise. The road to it is initially charming, passing through parklands around Shieldaig Bay and then continuing to the picturesque settlement of Badachro. Thereafter, the scenery deteriorates as a bleak moorland is crossed to the end of the road at Red Point where there is parking space for cars and a cairn and view-indicator nearby. The place is itself cheerless, its one great attraction being a wonderful seascape extending to Skye and the Outer Hebrides, with a landward view of the Torridon giants as a bonus.

Walkers may continue from Red Point on a clifftop walk to Diabaig on Loch Torridon (*see* p. 66). Proposals to replace this path with a motor road have been considered but happily pigeon-holed.

Above *Badachro Inn*

The view from Red Point

Loch Maree

Beyond the Badachro junction, the A.832 crosses an upland where an attractive loch, now a reservoir, invites a halt and a short walk on the paths around its shores. Then follows a long descent along a forest avenue to Loch Maree.

LOCH MAREE

Loch Maree is not just a pretty name. I think it is the loveliest of Scotland's freshwater lochs. A beautiful waterway twelve miles long and relatively narrow, Loch Maree occupies a long straight furrow between tawny hills and, from end to end, nothing mars the tranquillity of the scene. The road alongside, formerly a stop-and-start affair, is now a fast two-track road less in keeping with the surroundings and giving less opportunity to admire the passing scene.

Tributaries feed the loch from Glen Docherty, beyond Kinlochewe, and its waters escape into the River Ewe for a last short journey of two miles only to the sea. Between the two extremities, all is fair to look upon, serene and peaceful; copses of birch and alder and pines adorn the rocky heights alongside and the water's edge with occasional open views to the mountains bordering the far shore, along which the old track from Poolewe to Kinlochewe ran through the private estate of Letterewe. At the wider northern end of the loch, many islands break the surface.

After emerging from the forest, but still shaded by trees, the road passes the Loch Maree Hotel, proud of the fact that Queen Victoria stayed there, as a roadside plaque testifies. Offshore here is the Isle of Maree, a place of legendary prehistoric rites and ceremonies. Further on, the road crosses open moorland to arrive at Grudie Bridge, which is not now the delightful picnic spot it used to be, the old stone bridge having been replaced and many of the noble pines sacrificed to road widening; nothing, however, can diminish the majesty of Slioch directly across the water. Nearing the head of the loch, the road goes through the woodlands of the Beinn Eighe Nature Reserve and trails are available for the public up the mountainside. Then Kinlochewe is reached.

Opposite *Loch Maree from the nature reserve*   *Slioch*

KINLOCHEWE

Not many tourists pass this old staging post without stopping. It has changed little although modernised by a filling station and a caravan park and offers the only opportunity to spend money within a very wide area; there is also a long-established hotel popular with Victorian mountaineers, a shop and a café. Most visitors arrive in cars and coaches but it remains for walkers an excellent base for mountain expeditions, with major climbs in the immediate vicinity.

It is possible from the village, without too much effort, to survey the great wilderness of Fisherfield Forest from the east by taking the private road to the little huddle of buildings known as the Heights of Kinlochewe and thence following a rising track to the left until the vast amphitheatre is revealed in a surround of formidable mountains of which Slioch and Mullach Coire Mhic Fhearchair are now the most prominent. There is no sound, no movement. The whole scene is as lifeless as a huge painted canvas. This is wilderness country indeed.

TORRIDON

The very name of Torridon flutters the hearts of those who know and love this most exciting mountain area. A low pass carries a narrow road from Kinlochewe to the sea, and ranged along its northern side are the two huge masses of Beinn Eighe and Liathach, together extending in intimidating slopes over a distance of ten miles: Munros both, and among the best. They are all the more impressive because the road at their base nowhere attains much height, being lower than 350 feet above sea level at its summit. Thus they are seen in full stature, their crests being 3000 feet above the road, in an upthrust of unremitting steepness without a single weakness to encourage ascent. Beinn Eighe and Liathach are for heroes. A full day is required for either.

Torridon has appeal to other than mountaineers. There are admirers of rugged grandeur who are content merely to survey the scene from easy points of vantage. There are others who often do not leave their cars but are mightily impressed without recognising the various summits by name. And there are some who tremble with awe and hurry past. Torridon can never be ignored.

The A.896 road through the pass remains narrow with passing places, although a few parking spaces have been cut out of the verges to accommodate the many car owners who come to walk. A wide double carriageway here would be out of place and out of character. Torridon is right as it is.

Beinn Eighe across Loch Claire

Beinn Eighe is the great cornerstone of Torridon, overlooking both the pass and Loch Maree. It is more a range than a single mountain, having nine peaks linked by the graceful curves of supporting ridges. The distinctive off-white appearance of the crest and upper slopes, often mistaken for snow, is caused by a liberal covering of quartzite scree, the visual effect being of sterility and virgin purity. The vegetated lower slopes are a Nature Reserve providing sanctuary for creatures of the wild.

Seen from the road, the mountain is greatly foreshortened and its true proportions are best appreciated from a distance. The classic viewpoint is the far end of Loch Coulin, reached from the pass near Loch Clair on a private road to Coulin Lodge. This is a public right of way for walkers and it continues as a track alongside Loch Coulin, where camera enthusiasts are often fortunate to find a moored rowing boat posing for the foreground of a perfect picture. This is a beautiful short walk with rewards out of all relationship to effort.

Beinn Eighe

Liathach

Liathach is the greatest challenge to Torridon's visitors and only those of more than average energy and experience should accept it. This mountain looks a monster, its very steep acclivities soaring sky-ward in terraces of uncompromising cliffs seamed by scree-filled gullies and nowhere offering a restful stance, while the upper slopes and ridges are deserts of stones arduous to negotiate. Liathach is not only for heroes; masochists will revel in its punishments. It has little sympathy with intruders.

Like Beinn Eighe, it takes the form of a long ridge with several summits, its full traverse involving a major expedition that will live in the memory for ever. There is no way up that does not call for sustained effort, and while a thin track is forming from a cairn on the roadside and will be some help when well trodden, Liathach will never be an easy climb.

Liathach, like its neighbour, is best seen from a distance, a popular viewpoint being the private road to Coulin Lodge, where it towers as a great wedge across the waters of Loch Clair, after a short stroll from the pass road.

Coire Mhic Fhearchair

There is one walk, and one only, on the northern mountain façade of Torridon, available to walkers of average ability and, by a happy topographical coincidence, it leads to the natural feature most worth seeing. This is the wild recess of Coire Mhic Fhearchair which, due to recent publicity, has become a showplace to which conducted parties are taken. The corrie cradles a loch at the foot of a trinity of towering near-vertical buttresses of quartzite supported on a sandstone base: a spectacular and distinctive formation.

The way to it enters the obvious breach between Beinn Eighe and Liathach, reached from the top of the pass, a rough path climbing alongside the descending stream and then curving around the side of Sail Mhor, an outlier of Beinn Eighe, to the lip of the corrie and a sudden revelation of mural precipices on a grand scale. The distance there and back is eight miles and at least four hours should be allowed for comfort.

At the western end of the pass, here known as Glen Torridon, houses appear and there is an information centre, the immediate area being a popular tourist haunt. Loch Torridon is directly ahead and the road forks before reaching it, the through road continuing along the south shore and another branching along the north side and coming to a dead end at Diabaig after nine miles.

This secondary road offers a detour well worth making. It passes through Torridon, where there is a post office and a good shop. The small village appears to be under constant threat of a landslide from the steep slopes immediately behind. After passing a pier and following the water's edge for a mile, the road climbs to a higher level at a hairpin bend to avoid the private Torridon estate and, amongst trees, reaches a bridge with an adjacent car park. This is a place to halt.

The bridge spans the watercourse descending from Coire Mhic Nobuil in a very attractive setting, well seen from the parapet. A lovely path goes up alongside amongst trees and in a few minutes leads to the open corrie and an impressive mountain scene: directly ahead is Beinn Dearg, the high mass on the left is Beinn Alligin and on the right is the last satellite of the Liathach range. This short stroll is within the capacity of most car-bound travellers.

The car park over the bridge has been provided to accommodate the cars of those aspiring to climb Beinn Alligin, the track starting directly opposite. Beinn Alligin is the third of the great Torridon giants and more amenable than its fellows, and more honest, the whole effort of climbing to the summit ridge, traversing it and descending at the far end to return down the corrie being assessed at a glance, although probably under-estimated. The reward is a superlative panorama in all directions. A remarkable feature of the mountain is the tremendous gash on its eastern face, looking as though cut by a giant knife.

Beinn Alligin

Above *The view from the bridge*

Diabaig

Beyond the car park, the road contours the hillside, two branches going down to the coastal dwellings of Inver Alligin, and then turns sharply uphill to force a narrow passage across a bare and rocky headland on the last stage of its journey. In wild surroundings a natural amphitheatre containing two lochs is rounded and, just when the road seems to have lost direction and to be leading nowhere, there are signs of civilisation and cultivation, a perfect harbour is suddenly revealed and a steep descent ends at its terminus there. Diabaig is a surprise.

DIABAIG

The tiny port of Diabaig is charming, a miniature fit for framing. The pier is small, the cottages few and tidily arranged, the little beaches a delight for pebble collectors, the bay a narrow inlet of Loch Torridon landlocked on three sides by gaunt grey hills, and only the cry of seabirds disturbs the silence. Nothing seems to happen here, remote from the rest of the world, yet one of the houses supplies weather reports to the BBC and achieves for the community a frequent mention. One feature I was sad to see here on a recent visit was a fish hatchery installed in the bay, a sight now common in the western lochs and doubtless contributing to the local economy; sad because I feel that all living creatures should have freedom of movement and not be bred and confined in restricted space for the table. In these fish farms, maritime prisons, trout and salmon are doomed to swim around like goldfish in a bowl, denying them their inborn instinct to travel freely.

Diabaig is not quite the end of everything. A footpath leaves here on a lonely clifftop walk to Red Point for Gairloch, a magnificent trek with views across to the Outer Hebrides: *see also* p. 58.

On the return journey by road, there are glorious panoramas of the Torridon district, a large cairn indicating a popular viewpoint.

The shore of Loch Torridon at Diabaig

Torridon, from the Diabaig road

Below *Liathach from Loch Torridon*

Fuar Tholl

An Ruadh-stac　　　　　Below *Sgorr Ruadh*

COULIN FOREST

The south side of the Torridon pass is also entirely mountainous, with a sprinkling of Munros, although less intimidating and more inviting than the north flank.

This area is the Coulin Forest, bounded by roads that give it detachment from other high ground, its mountains forming a compact group but individually having distinction of character and outline, some being of arresting appearance. None of them yield easy climbs, the approaches being rough and the summits gained over pathless terrain liberally endowed with cliffs. What I particularly like about the Coulin heights is their rugged independence. Although a close-knit group and members of the same family, no two are alike, each posing its own problems of route finding, its own hazards; only in the excellence of their views are they akin.

The highest of them is Sgorr Ruadh and the next Maol Chean-dearg, both only fully revealed by walks into the interior of the Forest. The peak best known by sight is Fuar Tholl, in view from the Kyle–Dingwall railway at its base, where it towers threateningly over the line.

But all the mountains are worth seeing, whether climbed or not.

The charm of the Coulin Forest is best appreciated by walking through it. Some of the paths are closed during the shooting season but there is a right of way between the Torridon pass and Achnashellach, and it is a delight to follow. Walking from north to south, it starts along the private road to Coulin Lodge and continues past Loch Coulin as a good track, rising a little before descending through a forest of conifers to Achnashellach Station. Even better, but longer, is a track heading west from a meeting of waters a mile beyond Loch Coulin: this brings Sgorr Ruadh into full view, the route descending with its stream into Loch Coire Lair beneath the frowning precipice of Fuar Tholl to reach the rhododendrons of Achnashellach. This latter deviation can, of course, be used to make a circular walk from the station of about seven miles.

Another way into the interior is offered by a stalker's path from Annat at the head of Loch Torridon (closed in the later months of the year): this leads to the tarns at the foot of Maol Chean-dearg with a branch turning off to An Ruadh-stac. Beinn Damh, identified by a conspicuous horseshoe of scree high on its south side, is usually climbed by the long ridge coming up from Loch Torridon.

All expeditions in Coulin Forest are good.

Beinn Damh

Below *Maol Chean-dearg*   *Beinn na A' Eaglaise*

Beinn Alligin, from Loch Torridon

At the head of Loch Torridon, the main road coming from Kinlochewe turns along the south shore for Shieldaig, first passing through the settlement of Annat.

I once walked from Shieldaig to Annat long before the two communities were linked by a modern road, a woodland path pointing the way. I arrived at Annat in the early afternoon and was disappointed not to find any offers of refreshment on display. I cheekily went across to a detached cottage and asked if it was possible to get a bite to eat. Although taken aback, the lady invited me in. Her husband was sitting by the fire. He was very friendly and told me he was a cripple, unable to work, but he and his wife managed on a small pension; there was no bitterness in his voice. After a few minutes in the kitchen, the lady placed before me a plate of home-made scones, a dish of jam and a large pot of tea, all delicious. When the time came for me to pay and depart, my enquiry about the cost of the meal was brushed aside. 'Go on wi' ye,' said the lady with a happy smile that shed the years from her sad face. . . . Every time I have been in Annat since, I have remembered this further demonstration of Highland hospitality by people obviously poor in everything except the warmth of their welcome for strangers. I have never since been able to identify the cottage, but it was no hallucination. That simple repast was fit for a king.

The new road has opened up for motorists an area hitherto out of bounds. It rises high above the loch and its fringe of woodlands, and at its highest point is provided with car parks giving a magnificent view of Loch Torridon below and the exciting range of mountains beyond. The gem of the picture is Beinn Alligin directly opposite, and seen across the lovely environs of the loch: a perfect arrangement for the camera.

SHIELDAIG

The new road sweeps along an incline behind Shieldaig and a motorist intent on his gears may pass the village without noticing it. But although it is not now necessary to visit the long row of sea-front cottages, Shieldaig is far too good to be bypassed. It is delightfully situated at the head of Loch Shieldaig, an inlet of Loch Torridon, sheltered by rough hills, the whole picturesque scene encompassed by rocky heights. The cottages form a continuous line facing the water on one side of the street only, as is usual in the coastal villages. They all have a view to the greater expanse of Loch Torridon from their windows, although partly obstructed by the wooded Shieldaig Island. On a beautiful day, Shieldaig is a reminder of heaven.

The village is not quite the paradise it once was. The new and improved roads have attracted many tourists, with the inevitable consequences of commercial development: a hotel and restaurant, a filling station, B and B signs, caravans. But these are unobtrusive in the general pattern of Shieldaig and do not detract from its greatest appeal: its wonderful scenery in an incomparable setting.

When I first came to Shieldaig, I walked the twelve miles from Lochcarron in the south, on the only road giving access to the village, a road badly rutted and offering no invitation to wheels and, indeed, no vehicles passed me. I had noticed the name on the map; it seemed very remote but I had seen a reference to an inn there. When I arrived, the village was deathly quiet; a few fishing boats were pulled up on the shingly beach but there was no activity. I walked the length of the main street twice, looking for the inn or a place of refreshment. There was nothing. Shieldaig did not expect visitors and there was no welcome for strangers. I felt an intruder. When a native finally appeared, my enquiry about the inn was received with surprise. There had been an inn years ago but lack of support had closed its doors. I was directed to the house that had formerly been the inn and was admitted for an overnight stay with supper, bed and breakfast. The lady of the house lived alone, there were no callers; she was friendly but not communicative and the evening passed in silence.

Shieldaig today is very different in its habits. Visitors animate the street and are catered for, but only the quietness is disturbed and the village remains unspoiled. It is still a foretaste of heaven.

Shieldaig

Shieldaig and Torridon

Shieldaig now enjoys the extravagance of three through motor roads. Twenty years ago it had one only: the Lochcarron artery, and this is still the main supply route, now transformed into a fast highway. This passes through a mile-long avenue of noble Scots pines (denuded by a recent fire) soon after leaving the village, crosses a bare upland with views of the mountains of Coulin Forest, and is joined by a road from Applecross for the last stage of the journey to Lochcarron; our itinerary will join it at the junction after a tour of the Applecross peninsula which follows below. The second road, built mainly for tourist traffic, opened the way to Annat, Torridon and Kinlochewe.

The most recent road circuits the northern coast of the Applecross peninsula and branches from the Lochcarron road outside Shieldaig. The first mile is very pleasant and gives an exquisite view of the village backed by the mountains of Torridon: one of the most beautiful prospects in the country, a classic not yet well known.

THE APPLECROSS PENINSULA

The road heads north-west following the coast of Loch Torridon and passing occasional habitations and the village of Kenmore; this is situated on a pleasant bay where there is another fish hatchery. Then it continues across open and barren moorland to Fearnbeg, where it formerly ended. Some fifteen years ago, it was extended and now goes around the northern tip of the peninsula before turning south for a straight run down the west coast in bleak country, featureless except for the sad ruins of abandoned crofts yet relieved by glorious views across to Skye and the islands of the Inner Sound.

After many straight miles, the road curves inland to round Applecross Bay, a welcome sight well endowed with trees and, after passing a picnic place, turns into the village of Applecross, a friendly place with no obvious awareness of its extreme isolation from the rest of the world. The road continues south, passing other little settlements, to end at Toscaig Pier, a source of supply when winter snows block the high pass to Lochcarron.

Skye from the Bealach na Ba

Until the northern route was made the only road link between Applecross and the world outside lay over the notorious Bealach na Ba, a high and difficult pass attaining an elevation of 2000 feet; a sore trial for a timid car driver. The road rises steadily from Applecross for four miles to the summit of the pass; on level ground here a large car park has been provided for motorists who wish to halt and admire the superb view across to Skye on a clear day. I met a man here once who had made an annual pilgrimage to this spot for forty years.

The high altitude of the pass gives walkers an opportunity to visit the summits of the two mountains of Applecross without much extra climbing. Sgurr a' Chaorachain and Beinn Bhan rise to the north of the road, the latter being especially worth a visit for a dramatic view of the cliffs around the Coire na Feola.

Loch Kishorn from the Bealach na Ba

Below *Oilrig construction unit on Loch Kishorn*

Bealach na Ba

From the top of the Bealach na Ba a new landscape is seen ahead, Loch Kishorn, the next objective. It appears far below, framed by near-vertical cliffs on both sides of a vast hollow into which the narrow road plunges in a series of sharp zigzags. The descent needs great care through its fall of 500 feet; then the gradient eases and more confident progress can be made over a widening and declining moorland to the shore of Loch Kishorn. An access road branches off along the lochside to serve an oilrig construction unit, the weird contraptions of which are a disfigurement one hopes will be temporary.

Our road turns round the head of the loch to join the A.896 from Shieldaig. In the pleasant countryside around the roofless ruin of Courthill House (not destroyed by fire as may be supposed but dismantled by its owner to avoid paying rates), the road turns sharply east to enter a ravine where waterfalls are to be seen, and then climbs over a low ridge to descend to Lochcarron.

LOCHCARRON

Lochcarron, like Ullapool, is a village with the busy atmosphere of a town. Its mile-long street, continuously built up along the side facing the loch from which it gets its name, has many shops, banks, garages, hotels and guest houses, patronised by customers from a wide area and by the touring motorists who pass through and invariably halt. It has an air of prosperity, having recovered from the damage to its economy caused by the closing of the Strome Ferry and the re-routing of the main road on the far side of the loch. The compensating influences are the improved road to Shieldaig, a magnet for tourists, while the development of the oilrig installations on Loch Kishorn has resulted in a Klondyke-style boom in trade.

The open aspect of the village, positioned to enjoy day-long sunshine and spared the dominance of high mountains, suggests a calm and friendly environment, especially appreciated upon reaching it after travelling through the exciting scenery of the Highlands.

Lochcarron

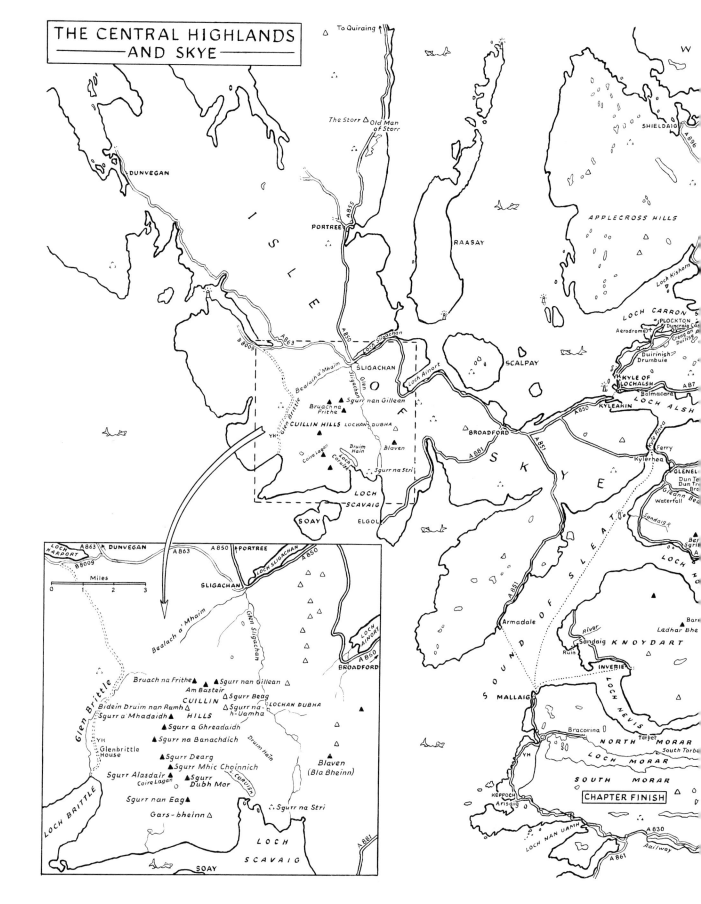

THE CENTRAL HIGHLANDS
AND SKYE

To Quiraing

The Storr △ Old Man
of Storr

DUNVEGAN

SHIELDAIG

A 896

APPLECROSS HILLS

Loch Kishorn

PORTREE

RAASAY

LOCH CARRON

PLOCKTON

Aerodrome

Duncraig Cas

Crea an a

Duirinish

I

S

L

E

SCALPAY

Duirinish
Drumbuie

KYLE OF
LOCHALSH

A 87

Balmacara

Loch Sligachan

SLIGACHAN

LOCH ALSH

Bealach a' Mhaim

Glen Sligachan

O

F

Loch Ainort

KYLEAKIN

A 850

Sgurr nan Gillean ▲

Bruach na
Frithe ▲

CUILLIN HILLS

LOCHAN DUBHA △

BROADFORD

A 851

Kyle Rhea

S

Ferry

Kylerhea

GLENEL

YH

Glen Brittle

Coire Lagan

Druim
Hain

Loch
Coruisk

Blaven

K

Y

E

Dun Te
Dun Tr
Brod
Gleann Bea

Waterfall

Sgurr na Stri

Sandaig R

Ber
Sgril

A

LOCH
SCAVAIG

SOAY

ELGOL

LOCH H

CHAPTER FINISH

Armadale

S

O

U

N

D

O

F

S

L

E

A

T

River

Sandaig

K N O Y D A R T

Ruin

Ladhar Bhe
Bare

INVERIE

S MALLAIG

LOCH NEVIS

Bracorina

Tarpet

NORTH
MORAR

South Torbe

Druim
Hain

Blaven
(Bla Bheinn)

LOCH MORAR

SOUTH
MORAR

KEPPOCH

YH

Arisaig

LOCH NAN UAMH

A 830

Railway

A 861

Inset map:

LOCH
HARPORT

A 863 DUNVEGAN

A 850 PORTREE

B 8009

LOCH SLIGACHAN

A 850

Miles
0   1   2   3

SLIGACHAN

Bealach a' Mhaim

Glen Sligachan

LOCH
AINORT

A 850

BROADFORD

Glen Brittle

Bruach na Frithe ▲

Am Basteir ▲

Sgurr nan Gillean ▲ △

△ Sgurr Beag

CUILLIN

LOCHAN DUBHA

Bidein Druim nan Ramh △

△ Sgurr na-
h-Uamha

Sgurr a Mhadaidh ▲

HILLS

Sgurr a Ghreadaidh ▲

Sgurr na Banachdich ▲

YH
Glenbrittle
House

Drum Hain

CORUISK

Sgurr Dearg ▲

Sgurr Mhic Choinnich ▲

Blaven
(Bla Bheinn)

Sgurr Alasdair ▲

Coire Lagan

Sgurr
Dubh Mor ▲

Sgurr nan Eag ▲

Gars-bheinn △

△ Sgurr na Stri

LOCH BRITTLE

LOCH
SCAVAIG

SOAY

A 881

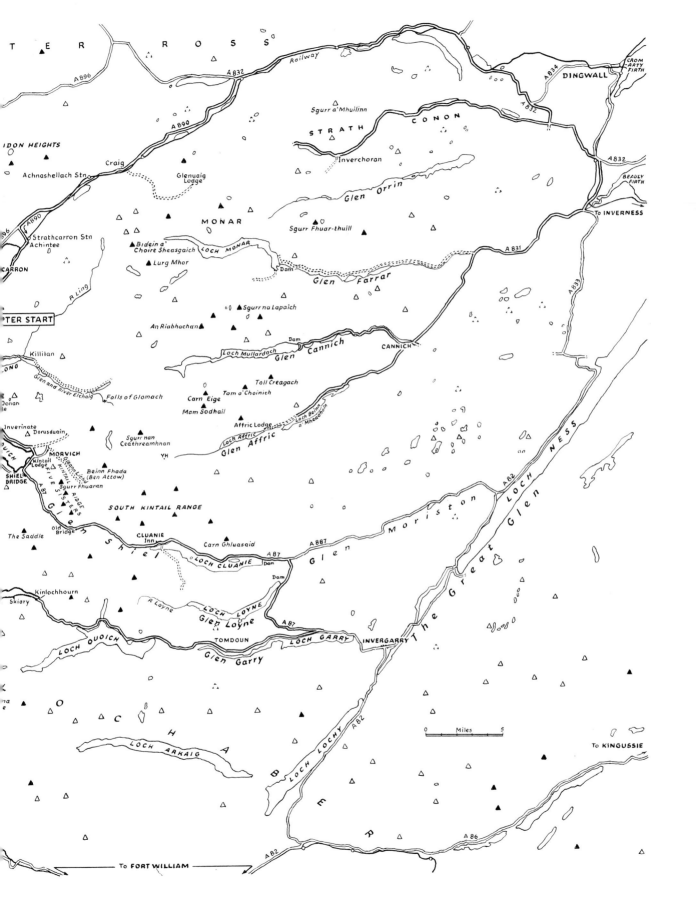

THE CENTRAL HIGHLANDS AND SKYE

LOCH CARRON is a sea loch, and a long one, extending some sixteen miles inland from the open sea. Formerly it was a watery barrier on the journey along the west coast, and the key to its crossing was the small car ferry at Stromeferry, a source of long delays and frustration, but the ferry was abandoned when a new road was constructed along the south-east shore of the loch. The once-important road from the ferry to Lochcarron village is now quiet and demoted; it joins the A.896 from Shieldaig at the entrance to the village, beyond which, with the new loch now behind, a new and important road junction is reached. This is the point where the re-routed A.890 comes in to resume its original course.

Here our itinerary takes us along the new section of the road, rather surprisingly signposted to Fort William, and brings us to the first railway so far seen, at Strathcarron Station. This is the line between Kyle of Lochalsh and Dingwall for Inverness, a vital link between west and east under threat of closure but still happily reprieved. The people of Wester Ross depend greatly on the trains for travel and supplies, and would be even more isolated without them; moreover, the railway proves a most enjoyable crossing of the Highlands scenically and is very popular with visitors. The last time I travelled on it there was standing room only. Closing it would be criminal folly.

Leaving the station at a level crossing, the road turns to follow the shore of Loch Carron towards the sea in the close company of the railway. The difficulties of constructing the road (and even more so the railway) are plain to see: much had to be cut out of the living rock, netted to arrest stonefalls, and at one point both pass through a tunnel. There was litigation after the completion of the road, the railway authorities claiming substantial compensation from the Highways authority for damage and disturbance to the railway track.

Nearing the narrows of the loch where the ferry operated, the road climbs a long incline through a forest, emerging in open country and here a branch, formerly the main road, goes down to the hotel and other buildings grouped forlornly around the old ferry pier: it is always sad to see an enterprise that has served its purpose well and has now had its day.

The A.890 now turns south to Loch Duich and, ultimately, as the signpost promised, to Fort William, bypassing the forestry village of Achmore. But Loch Duich must wait. Achmore is entered and from it goes a narrow road to Plockton and Kyle of Lochalsh on a journey of sustained delight.

Strathcarron railway station   *Road and rail tunnel*

Plockton and Loch Carron

The Kyle road from Achmore curves round to renew acquaintance with Loch Carron as it passes through the narrow straits of Strome and widens into an estuary. Also emerging beneath the cliffs of the narrows is the railway, resolutely maintaining a level contour despite all the difficulties of the terrain. It runs below a raised beach, evidence that in ages past the waters of the loch were higher than they are today. The railway continues to hug the coast and is lost to sight below the wooded slopes traversed by the road, which now becomes a fragrant avenue between trees and heathery banks spangled with primroses and, further, covered with rhododendrons. Occasionally, breaks in the foliage permit glimpses of the estuary and its islands, now a wide expanse with Loch Kishorn joining in and the Applecross hills forming a distant background: all exquisitely lovely.

Still narrow with passing places but very little traffic, the road passes below the impending cliffs of Creag an Duilisg, almost vertically overhead, and enters the environs of Duncraig Castle, a residential school of domestic science in a heavenly location – specimen trees, lawns and gardens combining to enhance the glorious view over the water. A headland is now seen jutting into the estuary with a line of white cottages fronting a bay. This is Plockton, soon to be visited.

Continuing, this charming road, my second favourite in all Scotland, now turns inland to avoid the high ground overlooking Plockton, and after a new byroad leaves on the right, makes a long detour, passing a pleasant inland loch, to arrive at a T-junction at Duirinish, the left fork heading for Kyle of Lochalsh, that on the right being a no-through-road to Plockton. The byroad mentioned is a short cut to Plockton, and a short walk from its highest point leads to a viewpoint commanding a magnificent prospect of the estuary backed by the Applecross and Torridon heights, and with an aerial view of sweet Plockton directly below. Let's go there.

Plockton

PLOCKTON

Dear Plockton! Throughout the 1970s, this delightful village was the priority holiday venue of my wife and myself, a kind friend providing her cottage for our annual visits: always we arrived in eager anticipation and departed with reluctance. Apart from its intrinsic charms, which are many, the village is a splendid centre for the exploration of Wester Ross and Skye and abounds in lovely walks nearby. Despite a growing influx of visitors, it has changed very little in the forty years since I first saw it, remaining unspoiled and unsophisticated. True, the black cows, apparently of no fixed abode, that used to saunter along the streets and back lanes, foraging and friendly, have gone, and Edmund MacKenzie has moved his shop to new premises, but otherwise Plockton today is as it has always been within my memory, and is best appreciated in the evenings when the day trippers have departed.

It is different: unlike most coastal villages on the western seaboard, it faces east, on a bay of Loch Carron, is well sheltered by a belt of trees on a high bank, has an equable climate that allows palms and exotic plants to flourish outdoors and enjoys immunity from heavy traffic and disturbance. The cottages, in a continuous line facing the water of the bay, have gardens across the street and a small peninsula across a causeway also has enviable residences.

Plockton started existence as a fishing port, and the old harbour can still be seen, but it is that no longer, pleasure sailing being the new order of the day; and visitors are catered for without fuss or ostentation. By common consent, it is the prettiest of Scotland's west coast villages and, although small, is well endowed with a large modern school serving a wide area, a railway station and even an airfield. There is a caravan park, mercifully hidden from the village street. It really deserves a more romantic name, Plockton meaning the town on the headland. But what's in a name? Plockton is a little paradise.

Kyle of Lochalsh is the next port of call, and the way to it from Plockton returns to the T-junction at Duirinish, turns along its main street and skirts the next village of Drumbuie, scene of a great hullabaloo two decades ago when a proposal to construct an oilrig installation off-shore was repulsed by spirited opposition, a home subsequently being found for it on an uninhabited shore of Loch Kishorn. From Drumbuie, a heathery moorland is crossed to join the old main road into Kyle, now superseded by another. Glorious views open up across the Inner Sound to Skye and smaller islands; road and railway jostle together on the last exciting mile to Kyle of Lochalsh.

Skye across the Inner Sound

The railway station at Kyle of Lochalsh

KYLE OF LOCHALSH

After the tranquillity of Plockton, Kyle of Lochalsh has the atmosphere of a bustling metropolis. Here is the terminus of the railway from Dingwall and Inverness, the pier where the large MacBrayne's boats call and short cruises depart and, most important for the local economy, the ferries ply across a narrow strait to the island of Skye: a very popular voyage of five minutes only but often achieved after a wait of hours in a queue. There are many commercial interests in Kyle and constant activity along the coastline: there are hotels, banks, shops, an information centre and even a gasholder to remind urban visitors of the life they have left.

The pier

The ferry across to Skye

I could never visit Kyle of Lochalsh without feeling an impelling urge to go across to Skye, and now, in writing this book, which was originally intended to be about the mainland only, I find that I simply cannot pass the island by without a further look at its highlight, the Black Cuillin. I justify this departure from intention by advancing a theory that Skye was obviously once a part of the mainland: a study of the map confirms that it is separated only by a narrow channel, Kyle Rhea, the configuration of the shores on either side matching as though torn apart in ages past. I may be wrong, but it is on this doubtful premise that we take the ferry and alight from it in Skye.

Opposite *Skye from the mainland*   *The Black Cuillin, from Sligachan*

THE BLACK CUILLIN OF SKYE

The ferry crosses to Kyleakin and from here a good modern road heads west, replacing a narrow and rough one that tested the car springs of the early visitors to the Cuillin. Keeping close to the coast, it arrives at the village of Broadford: thus far, the scenery is not inspiring, the hinterland being a dull moorland and the seaward views more pleasing. Beyond Broadford, the region of the Red Hills is by-passed and after rounding the head of Loch Ainort, the road comes alongside Loch Sligachan and turns inland to reveal a first sighting of the mystic spires of the Black Cuillin, the grandest mountains in all Britain – a journey of twenty-five miles from the ferry. From Sligachan, only the northern end of a compact mass of peaks and pinnacles, linked by a high ridge of naked rock, can be seen, but by a circuitous byroad, the main climbing centre of Glen Brittle may be reached. The few miles between bring into view other arresting features of a fantastic skyline which bristles with Munros in the shape of abrupt towers of rock poised above precipitous cliffs and deep corries. It is a scene, both compelling and repelling, that will never be forgotten. The Black Cuillin are the stuff of which ambitions are made. And dreams. And nightmares.

Below *The Basteir Tooth*

The ridge south from Bruach na Frithe

The Black Cuillin are not for ordinary mortals. Many of the summits can be reached but only by desperate scrambling.

There is one summit, however, that can be attained by red-blooded fellwalkers and, by great good fortune, it happens to be a magnificent belvedere for appraising the surroundings. It has a comprehensive view of the ridge and spectacular views of the fangs and pinnacles of rocks characteristic of this unique range.

This accommodating and recommended summit is Bruach na Frithe, reached from Sligachan by a path leaving the pedestrian track over the Bealach a' Mhaim; it is safe, without hazards, and calls for no more effort than the ascent of Scafell Pike in the English Lake District.

Probably the peak most often ascended is Sgurr nan Gillean, its shapely and challenging pyramid being prominent in the view from Sligachan. This fine mountain is defended by cliffs, the preserve of rockclimbers, but there is a tourist route within the ability of most active walkers. This skirts the base of the pinnacled north ridge and reaches a ridge beyond, where the final stage of the ascent, of daunting aspect, requires a very steep scramble up a narrowing spire to its airy top.

I came here with a companion in 1954, determined to conquer this graceful peak and thus set the seal on my mountaineering achievements but, to our shame, we shirked the last thirty yards to the summit cairn in growing apprehension of an instant demise. I kicked myself all the way back to the hotel for being an arrant coward, and next day persuaded my companion to return with me to the scene of our defeat and try again. This time, we succeeded and indeed met no difficulties apart from one awkward step across a gap just before the cairn. This time I patted myself on the back all the way to the hotel.

I rate the summit of Sgurr nan Gillean as the finest in my experience. The immediate surroundings are dramatic and spectacular in the extreme, with precipices falling away on all sides: it is exhilarating to be there, exciting, a little frightening yet one is aware of a rare privilege. And the views of the ridge and the sea beyond are breathtaking. No king ever sat on a prouder throne than I that day.

Glen Sligachan offers another worthwhile expedition that can be made easy or arduous according to taste.

Gentle ramblers, content with three or four miles, will find the path pleasant, with no climbing, and be rewarded with impressive views of the impending mountains. Average walkers will go further along the glen to the Lochan Dubha at the foot of Blaven before returning happily after a most interesting ten-mile trek.

Strong walkers will proceed beyond the Lochan Dubha and climb the easy ridge of Druim Hain directly facing until reaching a well-built obelisk commanding a sensational view of Loch Coruisk in a surround of wild mountains.

Super walkers will continue beyond the obelisk to the minor peak of Sgurr na Stri, overlooking Loch Scavaig and the open sea. A wonderful view of most of the Cuillin skyline.

Adrenalin runs fast in the Cuillin and eagerness keeps the feet moving, but it must be borne in mind that the miles are long and rough and enough time must be allowed for the return to base.

Sgurr nan Gillean

Above are illustrations of sections of the central ridge of the Cuillin. The traverse of the ridge from end to end is a challenge exclusively for equipped and experienced cragsmen, progress along it being possible only by arduous scrambling and rockclimbing. There is one short walk, however, that all visitors should make: this is the well-trodden path leading up into Coire Lagan from Glen Brittle. The corrie is an awe-inspiring amphitheatre below a ring of peaks that rise like cathedrals, their rock architecture being very spectacular. Here are Nature's skyscrapers.

Coire Lagan

Skye has no other scenic attractions to compare with the Black Cuillin but deserving of special mention is the capital, Portree, a bonny little town, and further north along the coast the Storr and its Old Man, conspicuous on the skyline. Beyond, the bizarre formations of the Quiraing, a strange assembly of spires and needles of rock that makes the beholder doubt the evidence of his eyes.

Whether time permits or not, a detour should be made along the A.881 from Broadford to its terminus at Elgol, there going down to the colourful beach of pebbles and wild flowers and low cliffs: a beautiful foreground to a classic view, the finest in Britain, of the Black Cuillin across the wide waters of Loch Scavaig, a picture that would defeat a Constable or a Turner.

View from Elgol

Above *The head of Loch Long*

Back on the mainland the new road from Kyle of Lochalsh, the A.87, closely follows the shore of Loch Alsh, making unnecessary the extra miles of the old route, and when they meet at Balmacara, the channel of Kyle Rhea is clearly seen across the water, the mainland confronting Skye and both doing their best to support my theory that they were once joined here like Siamese twins. Two miles further on, the A.890 from Loch Carron comes down to an improved junction. After two more miles, formerly lined with yellow flag iris but now destroyed by 'improvements', a side road branches off to Killilan along the beautiful banks of Loch Long.

THE FALLS OF GLOMACH

The public road to Killilan has for long been the usual route taken by motorists wishing to see the Falls of Glomach, permission to use a private road continuing into Glen Elchaig being a formality. At the end of the public road is a notice prohibiting cars from going further, and I am told that the new owners of the Killilan estate are enforcing this ban fairly strictly but not in all cases. It might therefore be worth trying to get permission and, if granted, the private road can be followed on a rough surface for five miles.

Then cars may be parked on the verges and a way made across a footbridge over the River Elchaig to a well-blazed path leading up, in one mile, to the top of the Falls of Glomach, a very popular objective of walkers approaching from the head of Loch Duich. It is unfortunate that both paths arrive at the head of the 350-foot falls where only the top plunge can be seen; the steep slope alongside may be descended, with care, to bring more of this splendid waterfall within camera range.

The Falls of Glomach

Eilean Donan Castle

DORNIE

Resuming the A.87 at the Killilan junction, the road now turns between banks ablaze with gorse and enters the populated environs of Dornie, bypassing the separate community of Ardelve and reaching the village over a long road bridge.

Dornie is situated at the point where Loch Alsh branches into two and loses its name, continuing as Loch Duich and Loch Long. Within the living memory of the older inhabitants of Dornie, there have been radical changes affecting both these waterways. There was a car ferry across the narrows of Loch Long, a source of delay on the journey to Kyle and Skye in pioneering days: this was replaced by the present road bridge earlier this century, and passage through Dornie, once slow and halting, is now swift. And there was a passenger ferry across Loch Duich from Totaig on the opposite shore, saving fourteen miles of road travel; this too has been abandoned.

But the great tourist attraction of Dornie remains. The romantic and historic stronghold of Eilean Donan Castle stands on a rocky promontory of Loch Duich, connected to the shore by a picturesque causeway of arches. The present impregnable appearance of the castle is due to a major restoration in the early years of this century, but there have been fortified buildings on this site since the days of the Viking invaders. The castle is open to the public on payment of an admission charge and has a most interesting interior with rooms beautifully furnished in medieval style. It is a compulsive stop for cars and coaches, the large parking places on the roadside often being taxed to capacity, but despite the inevitable crowds, Eilean Donan should be on the itinerary of all who pass this way.

The A.87 passes alongside, having been cut out of rocks to follow the shoreline. The old road, now known as the Scenic Route, climbs steeply out of Dornie and soon provides a magnificent aerial view of the castle and the loch with the hills of Skye in the background.

Loch Duich

The Scenic Route from Dornie is delightful, enjoying views denied to the modern A.87. It rises steadily to a height of almost 600 feet above the loch before levelling out at the top of a headland; cars may be parked here and a short stroll reveals an extensive panorama of exquisite beauty without a discordant note. The head of Loch Duich is in view backed by the Kintail ridge of Five Sisters and the Saddle with its satellites. Flanked by woodlands and forests below rocky hillsides, the full length of the loch is seen, merging into Loch Alsh with, beyond, the distant hills of Skye: a picture of perfection. I could sit here for hours, just looking.

The old road then descends to join the new. The village of Inverinate is bypassed and the head of Loch Duich reached as a green strath opens up ahead. The A.87 now crosses the loch on a long causeway with a warning of high winds, but even in calm weather the former road continuing up the valley to round the head of the loch, at the cost of two extra miles, is to be preferred. From this, a lane goes forward to the last habitation, Dorusduain, with a parking space midway. This is the start of the walkers' way to the Falls of Glomach, first up a forest road to cross a ridge and then gradually declining to the top of the waterfall. This is also the only way for motorists who have been refused permission at Killilan to use the private road, or who didn't like to ask, and are fit enough to do eight miles there and back on foot.

The former road turns beyond the lane junction and crosses the valley to Morvich, a farming settlement in lovely surroundings with accommodation and camping for the many walkers who find this a convenient base for their mountain expeditions.

Beinn Fhada

Morvich is situated at the foot of the vast Beinn Fhada, also known as Ben Attow, a rough-topped mountain seven miles long and of considerable girth. This massive upthrust stands athwart the main watershed of the Highlands, its waters draining west into Loch Duich and the Atlantic, and east into Glen Affric with an ultimate destination in the North Sea.

Two paths leave the Morvich area for Glen Affric. One leads up an unfrequented glen occupied by wild goats and skirts the northern flank of Beinn Fhada to arrive at a rough bealach or col, where I once shivered for two hours waiting for the mist to lift off Sgurr nan Ceathreamhnan ahead, which it did not. I regret I cannot give the correct pronunciation of the Gaelic names of the mountains: I never mastered them, adopting instead roughly similar English equivalents; thus, for example, Ceathreamhnan to me was Chrysanthemum. . . . This path, if continued over the bealach, descends into the wild upper reaches of Glen Affric.

The other route, a very popular one with hardy walkers, goes along Gleann Lichd, pleasantly wooded in its lower parts and ascends along the southern side of Beinn Fhada, with striking views of the Five Sisters opposite, to a bealach from which Glen Affric is seen ahead and easily reached. The through walk from Morvich to Cannich at the far end of Glen Affric is a classic marathon, a long day's march through changing landscapes and between impressive mountain ranges, ending amid scenes of sylvan beauty. Few dispute that Glen Affric is the loveliest of Scotland's valleys. And there are neighbouring glens on the east side of the watershed, also lovely and deserving of special mention. They cannot be omitted from this book.

At this stage of the itinerary I propose to suspend the journey south and visit the eastern glens. We will return to Morvich a few pages further on.

THE EASTERN GLENS

The glens of the north-west that carry their waters eastwards to Cromarty Firth and Beauly Firth each have individual character yet have features common to all. They follow roughly parallel courses down from high mountains to the coastal plain; all have lochs serving as reservoirs; all have roads, public or private, that extend far into the interior and there end; none of them is accessible by road from the west and they can only be approached by wheeled traffic coming from the east. But their differences are greater than their similarities and the four glens now to be described are all worthy of leisurely exploration and indeed make delightful excursions.

Most northerly of the four glens is Strath Conon in the district of Monar, favoured by having a public road throughout its length of twenty miles. It is quiet, pleasant, unexciting, but there is a good walk near the end of it where, from the farm of Inverchoran, a path goes up a side glen to reach a ridge giving a splendid view across the desolate Glen Orrin to Sgurr Fhuar-thuill and companion heights of Glen Farrar. The best view in Strath Conon is provided by the peaked summit of Sgurr a' Mhuilinn.

Strath Conon

Waterfall near Loch Monar

Permission must be obtained to travel by car along the private road in Glen Farrar and, if granted, should be regarded as a great privilege for there is loveliness all the way to its terminus at Loch Monar, now a reservoir. A short walk south from the dam brings two lofty peaks, Sgurr na Lapaich and An Riabhachan, into intimate view, and from the side of the loch there is a captivating glimpse, in a frame of pines, of distant mountains ahead across its waters.

At the head of Loch Monar is a cluster of Munros better approached from Craig, near Achnashellach on the A.890, where a forest road leads up to open deer pastures and continues as a rough cart track to Glenuaig Lodge in the heart of the mountains. Another route for walkers leaves Achintee near Strathcarron Station and ascends to a ridge overlooking the upper glen of the River Ling, where the shy twins, Bidein a' Choire Sheasgaich and Lurg Mhor, rarely seen, are fully revealed.

Neither of these exhilarating walks, however, rivals Glen Farrar in beauty of surroundings. Pray for permission.

The wooded environs of Glen Cannich add to the pleasure of travel on the public road to the great dam of Loch Mullardoch. The loch, like many others in the Highlands, is no longer as Nature fashioned it, the length having been increased from four to nine miles as the result of reservoir operations. It lies deep-set between high mountain ranges, that on the south side culminating in Carn Eige – at 3877 feet, the highest mountain north of the Great Glen. The raising of the water level has partially submerged a conspicuous pointed rock of historic interest; in the days of long ago, this was a meeting place of the Chisholm clan.

Best known of the eastern glens, with a deserved reputation for the variety and beauty of its landscapes, is Glen Affric, a long straight cutting through the mountains that provides a connecting link between east and west for travellers on foot. The through route of some twenty miles ranks amongst the finest walks in the Highlands for sustained interest. It extends south-west from the village of Cannich. A public road threads a delightful passage through woodlands in the company of river and loch for the first few miles, ending at a car park from which further progress is possible only by walking – and further progress should certainly be made.

At this point, a side glen comes in on the right with a path leading to the dominating heights of Carn Eige and Mam Sodhail, or from it the bealach between Tom a' Choinich and Toll Creagach may be reached and a fine view seen over Glen Cannich to the mountains of Glen Farrar.

The main route, however, continues up the glen on a private road, crossing the river and passing Affric Lodge and the shapely peak of Sgurr na Lapaich towering behind, to reach Loch Affric. This is a lovely sheet of water amongst trees, having as a powerful background the massive build-up of ridges leading up to the summit of Mam Sodhail, a major Munro 3862 feet high. The road, now a rough lane, continues beyond Loch Affric into more open country with mountains on both sides. Distantly ahead is seen Beinn Fhada, the key to the watershed crossing to Loch Duich, the bealach giving access to Gleann Lichd and Morvich but still half a day's march away. Miles are long in Glen Affric, but every one is a joy to walk.

Sgurr na Lapaich across Loch Affric

Loch Duich and the Five Sisters

KINTAIL AND KNOYDART

From Morvich, where we suspended our journey south on page 93, the old road turns south to join the A.87 coming over the causeway on Loch Duich and after passing through a huge cutting arrives at Shiel Bridge, a pleasant wooded oasis sheltered by high mountains. Here the A.87 goes forward into Glen Shiel, heading for places south, but before following it a detour to Glenelg and Loch Hourn is strongly recommended. These are isolated places dependent for a lifeline on the road from Shiel Bridge and otherwise quite inaccessible overland by vehicles. This road had a greater significance in past centuries when it was the regular route to Skye, the way taken by Dr Johnson and Boswell in their tour of exploration; a glance at the map shows that it followed a direct line from Shiel Bridge to Broadford across the Kylerhea ferry. It fell from favour when the railway came to Kyle of Lochalsh and the ferry there was developed: modern roads have since made this alternative approach much easier and avoid the high crossing of the Mam Ratagan Pass on the old route.

The road out of Shiel Bridge runs along the south side of Loch Duich and soon arrives at a junction where a no-through-branch turns off to serve the scattered habitations along the shore, ending at Totaig and the forlorn slipway of the abandoned ferry to Dornie. On the way back there is a glorious view ahead of the Five Sisters: if only to witness so lovely a scene, this detour within a detour is worth the extra half-hour.

From the junction, the road to Glenelg climbs steadily through a mature forest, winding in curves to ease the gradient. This section is not as deprived of light nor as gloomy as it once was, tree felling and gale damage having left gaps through which there are glimpses of the loch below, and the road has been cured of the hazards that beset the early travellers. There are no problems for modern cars and on an open hillside above the treeline, a roadside parking space has been provided where they can foregather and let their occupants feast on a superlative view of the head of Loch Duich and the Five Sisters.

This is the Mam Ratagan Pass, 1100 feet above Shiel Bridge.

Above *Kylerhea ferry*

Over the top of the pass there is a long descent through plantations and along a hillside into the fertile valley of Glen More, a quiet cultivated strath where a few farms keep their pastures in good heart, contrasting with the shaggy heights around. The first habitations of Glenelg are passed and the road forks.

KYLERHEA

The right fork is the old way to Skye, reaching the ferry for Kylerhea two miles further and ending there. The ferry takes cars and operates only in the summer months but, at busy times when the more popular crossing at Kyle of Lochalsh is subject to lengthy delays, this smaller ferry at Kylerhea may still provide the quickest route to the island. At this point, the channel is little more than a quarter of a mile wide and on the far bank a road continues the journey to Broadford.

The left fork goes on to the village of Glenelg and in a field between the two roads a gaunt ruin will be noticed: this in its eighteenth-century heyday was the barracks occupied by Hanoverian troops.

Above *The ruined barracks*

GLENELG

Glenelg is a small village but a complete one, having a church, a post office, a garage, a hotel, a shop, a café and a fine war memorial good enough to grace a London street. Glenelg overlooks the Sound of Sleat, an arm of the sea connected with Loch Alsh by the narrow channel of Kyle Rhea. There is a small harbour, and skeletons of boats decorate the stony beach, the road coming alongside after passing between the terraced cottages of the village.

The beach at Glenelg

Above *The broch of Dun Telve*

THE BROCHS OF GLEANN BEAG

The road beyond Glenelg turns a corner into Gleann Beag, reaching a junction where it crosses a river bridge and a minor road continues up this lovely valley. This no-through-road should certainly be followed, preferably on foot. It is an avenue of delight between fragrant hedges and bonny braes and in two miles leads to the ancient broch of Dun Telve, one of the best preserved of the hundreds of brochs in Scotland. These, built as defences against the Viking invaders, are accredited to the Iron Age and were skilfully constructed to a circular plan, with a double wall enclosing a stairway and a circular paddock for cattle. Dun Telve is now in Government care: much remains intact but a large part of its stone was robbed by local farmers in centuries past. It may be inspected by entering a low doorway.

A little further along the road is Dun Trodden, another broch in a more ruinous condition. On the far side of the valley and in sight of the approach to Dun Telve, a great waterfall plunges down a hillside, providing a spectacle, especially in spate, that puts even the Falls of Glomach to shame.

Back on the main road, it turns right at the junction in Gleann Beag, passing a complex of handsome farm buildings, and ascends a long incline where much-needed improvements have taken place. The road maintains a high level above the Sound of Sleat, although views are obstructed in places by dense conifer plantations.

Above *Waterfall in Gleann Beag*; below *The memorial stone at Camusfearna*

CAMUSFEARNA

Nearing the Sandaig River, which rushes down from the mountains and passes beneath the road to enter the Sound, gated forest roads lead down to the beach where Gavin Maxwell had a cottage he called Camusfearna and wrote his world best-seller about his life there with the sea otters he admitted to his home as companions. Gavin is dead; Camusfearna was demolished after he left, a single memorial stone marking the site; the otters come no more. Only the ring of bright water remains.

Arnisdale

The road continues on a switchback course, reaching more open ground with wider views and, after a few more miles that seem to be leading nowhere, arrives at the top of a hill where the cottages of Arnisdale are suddenly revealed around a bay ahead. The waters now seen are those of Loch Hourn, an inlet of the Sound of Sleat extending ten miles inland and, in its narrow further reaches, the most impressive of the western sea lochs. The road descends the hill and passes along the garden fronts of the houses. All is quiet; nothing stirs. There is no offering of material pleasures to visitors; not even a cup of tea. This is an insular community, its only link with the rest of the world being the lonely Glenelg road.

A mile beyond Arnisdale the road comes to a full stop at the crofts of Corran, the last outpost of civilisation; beyond is a mountain wilderness.

From Corran, it is possible to reach Kinlochhourn at the head of the loch by a footpath climbing around the steep hill rising behind. There is no way to this destination along the lochside through the narrows, but for the first two miles from the beach at Corran, beloved by oystercatchers, an enchanting path closely follows the shore in very impressive surroundings and a succession of delightful rocky coves and flowery nooks and patches of shingle. Few people come this way. I once found the complete skeleton of a sea otter here, a sad reminder of Camusfearna: could this have been one of Gavin's friends?

Both the two great mountains near Loch Hourn can be seen clearly from the beach at Corran. Beinn Sgritheall, or Sgriol, rises like a huge wedge in the sky immediately behind Arnisdale and, across the water, the Knoydart giant, Ladhar Bheinn, exhibits a wild grandeur.

The return to Shiel Bridge can only be made along the same road. There is no other.

Beinn Sgritheall

Below *The beach at Corran*

Sgurr Fhuaran

GLEN SHIEL

I always experience a pleasurable thrill when travelling along Glen Shiel. To me, when coming from the south, it means the beginning of the best, the gateway to the wonderful western seaboard, a region of lochs and glens and hills I have come to know so well after forty years of exploratory visits. Familiarity never breeds contempt here, only a growing affection. I am an exile returning.

The A.87 enters Glen Shiel at Shiel Bridge and after a level two miles in which the scenery is dominated by the highest of the Five Sisters, Sgurr Fhuaran seen in full stature, starts the gradual ascent to Cluanie, bypassing the old Bridge of the Spaniards, so called because of a battle here in 1719 between Redcoats and Jacobites, the latter being reinforced by Spanish troops. Below this bridge are fine cascades; above it the descending stream is crossed by a new bridge, the road then keeping in close company, the stream being tunnelled in places to prevent encroachment on the highway.

The glen is deeply enclosed by lofty mountain ranges, each side formed of a succession of peaks linked by ridges. For the collector of Munros, the skyline boundaries of Glen Shiel provide exhilarating expeditions with Munros so profuse that they can be picked off like apples from a tree. The north side is formed by the Five Sisters, four being above the qualifying 3000 feet; on the south side, they are even more prolific, seven Munros in a line, with two more better approached from Shiel Bridge. These are magnificent ridge walks quite apart from the reward of a bagful of Munros, but they are long and arduous and for experienced hillwalkers only. The hard work can be minimised by starting at the Cluanie end of the glen, which has the advantage of 800 feet in height.

On the journey up the glen, where there are some conifer plantations, the Five Sisters ridge appears foreshortened and cannot be seen in perspective, the individual summits being difficult to distinguish; those on the south side are rather more distant and better discerned. There are stalkers' paths but walking on the hills is discouraged in the deer-shooting season.

Don't forget the camera. Spectacular scenes abound in this lovely glen, the most-photographed being above the new bridge where there is a classic alpine view of the Saddle, a splendid mountain I have always had a soft spot for because I can pronounce its name with confidence.

The Saddle

My first visit to Glen Shiel, however, was not a happy one. I left Tomdoun in Glen Garry one morning intending to walk to Dornie. In those days, the road leaving Tomdoun was the only way over to Cluanie and Glen Shiel from the south: it crossed the River Loyne and climbed over an intervening ridge before descending to Cluanie. This road was subsequently abandoned, being partly submerged by the new Loch Loyne reservoir, and was replaced by another constructed some miles to the east.

I had not gone far before the rain started and it soon became a sluicing downpour that never abated all day. My only protection was a battered trilby and an old raincoat that soon admitted defeat. Cagoules and other modern waterproofs, so efficient today, had not then been invented. The unremitting four-mile ascent to the high pass over the ridge reduced me to a walking wet rag; I was literally soaked to the skin and could feel rivulets chasing each other down my bosom. The prospect of a hot lunch at the Cluanie Inn kept me going, but on arrival there, after ten miles of misery, I was dismayed to find the place closed and nobody in sight. The next habitation was a further ten miles away, at Shiel Bridge. I was devastated; I swore I would never come to Scotland again. I had a damp cigarette in the shelter of a doorway – but there was nothing to be gained by hanging about here and I set off, squelching at every step, along the road to Shiel Bridge. I saw nothing of the scenery; visibility was down to fifty yards. I was near the Bridge of the Spaniards when a car overtook me and stopped, the door was opened and a very friendly fellow at the wheel invited me in. I declined with thanks and waved him on: I had only two more miles to walk to Shiel Bridge and couldn't get any wetter and didn't want to repay his kindness by spraying water all over his car. It seems remarkable now, when Glen Shiel is so busy, that I had not seen a car nor a human being since leaving Tomdoun eighteen miles earlier. . . .

I could not find any accommodation at Shiel Bridge. Since Dornie was now out of the question, I went on to the Kintail Lodge Hotel, where I was admitted and taken up to a single room which, mercifully, was furnished with an electric fire. I was two hours too early for dinner and so spent the interval in a cloud of steam with my wet clothes draped around the fire. When they were no more than damp, I went down to dinner. To my dismay, the residents' lounge was full of people and one man was addressing the company, whether they liked it or not, with an account of his mountaineering adventures. This monologue went on throughout dinner, after which he insisted that we all went across the road to the village hall where he would show us his slides of the Lake District. Dutifully we went. His slides were good and his descriptions fairly accurate, but I sensed we were all glad to get back to the comfort of the hotel and I to my electric fire. By a coincidence I met this man on the summit of Sergeant Man in the Lake District two months later. He looked at me as though he had seen me somewhere before, but I passed by with a curt nod. There was to be no monologue that day.

Cluanie Inn

CLUANIE

The lonely inn at Cluanie has prospered since it served as a beerhouse for itinerant and infrequent travellers and today is a compulsive stop for cars and coaches. It stands on the slight and indefinite watershed at the head of Glen Shiel and has its own group of Munros in the high country dividing it from Glen Affric to the north. The old road to Tomdoun leaves here but is gated and closed to traffic. Over the watershed, the A.87 runs alongside Loch Cluanie, now a reservoir, below the steep slopes of more Munros; on the summit of one of them, Carn Ghluasaid, I disturbed the only ptarmigan I have ever seen. In calm clear weather, the mountains of the South Kintail Range are mirrored perfectly in the waters of the loch.

Beyond the dam, a road junction is reached. Here the new road over to Glen Garry, continuing the A.87 classification, turns to the right, the signpost still urging a visit to Fort William. The road going forward from the junction is the A.887, leading through Glen Moriston to the Great Glen. The A.87 climbs to the brow of a hill, passing the dam of the Loyne reservoir, and reveals from the roadside a full-length view of Glen Loyne and the splendid mountains grouped around its upper reaches.

Loch Loyne

Over the hill, Glen Garry comes into sight ahead and at a parking place indicating a viewpoint there is a magnificent panorama of this beautiful glen, more water than land, extending to a fine array of the Knoydart peaks on the western horizon.

The road descends to valley level in lovely birch woods and reaches a junction where the old road for Tomdoun and Kinlochhourn turns off. It is a twenty-mile drive to Loch Hourn at the end of this road, and twenty back, but it should be done at least once in a lifetime, the scenery being outstanding. Tomdoun, once a staging post on the road to the Isles but cruelly bypassed by the new road, is the last outpost, the road continuing and coming alongside the enlarged Loch Quoich where an isolated clump of rhododendrons is all that remains of Glenquoich Lodge. On both sides are high mountains, but the gem of the view is across the water to the south-west where the wild heights of Knoydart and Morar form an arresting skyline, the shapely pyramid of Sgurr na Ciche being most prominent.

Glen Garry   Below *Loch Quoich*

Kinlochhourn

KINLOCHHOURN

Finally the road turns away and makes a long and rough descent, with Loch Hourn dramatically in view ahead, to the few buildings of Kinlochhourn where there *is* life but no sign of it. A deathly hush envelops the scene, a silence that seems almost sinister. There is a brooding oppressiveness here that induces a feeling of unease.

However, having come thus far by car, exercise for the legs is needed, and a path along the south shore of the loch may be followed to the abandoned village of Skiary, wholly in ruins: a sad emphasis of the desolation around.

Most visitors will be glad to return to the friendlier atmosphere of Glen Garry where, rejoining the A.87, Invergarry and the Great Glen are soon reached.

THE ROUGH BOUNDS

South of Loch Hourn is the wilderness of Knoydart known as the Rough Bounds, a region entirely without motor roads and having only a few lonely and unfrequented tracks through the mountain fastnesses. Knoydart is a closed book for motorists and for all except walkers equipped with map and compass – and it is even difficult for strong walkers. The area is bisected by a track between Barrisdale on Loch Hourn, reached by a path from Kinlochhourn, and the village of Inverie on Loch Nevis, but Inverie can be reached or left only by boat. Knoydart is not exactly a no-go area but should be entered with caution.

For non-mountaineers, the great feature of Knoydart is Loch Nevis, forming its southern boundary. Like Loch Hourn, which in configuration it resembles closely, Loch Nevis is an inlet of the Sound of Sleat, initially wide but becoming narrow as it thrusts through the hills. Access to its remote upper reaches is invariably made by boat from Mallaig, a voyage rewarded by an intimate view of the beautiful peak of Sgurr na Ciche, towering immediately from the head of the loch.

Across Loch Nevis is Morar.

The silver sands of Morar

MORAR

Morar, like neighbouring Knoydart, is wild and inhospitable, without roads in the interior and similarly featuring a loch that pierces the mountain barrier over a distance of twelve miles. But there are two differences: Morar has a tourist fringe and its loch is of fresh water.

Loch Morar bisects the area, dividing North Morar from South Morar. At the seaward end, it is no more than a good stone's throw from the Atlantic beach but at a higher level, its issuing stream descending through a short wooded ravine to join the waters of the ocean. The narrow neck of land between loch and sea is crossed by a road and a railway that end three miles further at Mallaig. There are hotels and residences along this coastal road which has beautiful views across to the islands of Rum and Eigg, but the popular attraction hereabouts is the lovely strand of silver sand on the beach.

Loch Morar is a freak of nature. It occupies a long trench caused by a geological fault and is over a thousand feet deep, a much greater depth than the sea into which it debouches.

Some years ago, a local man reported an encounter with a monster while fishing in the loch and was positive about it but no further sightings have since been claimed.

Loch Morar

Opposite *The harbour, Mallaig* *Loch nan Uamh*

MALLAIG

Mallaig is the metropolis of the district. It is a fishing port of sufficient importance to justify the laying of a single track railway to it from Fort William, this passing through scenery of such exquisite beauty that it is widely acknowledged to be the most delightful railway in Britain. Mallaig is a village with the vitality and industry of a busy town, the main interest being centred on the harbour and the pier and the fish sheds where the sky is obscured by hundreds of screaming seagulls. Mallaig is the terminus of land: beyond, all travel is over water; there are regular sailings to Armadale in Skye and Kyle of Lochalsh, and more casual trips to Loch Nevis and the islands.

Behind the village is an undulating hinterland of barren foothills. I climbed the highest of these one day when Mallaig was too crowded with visitors for my liking and suffered my only experience of hostility from a Highlander. I was returning along a path and, when passing an isolated croft, a man and his sheepdog emerged. He shouted something unintelligible and ordered his dog to go and get me – which it did, giving me a painful nip on the back of the calf. Using strong language I seldom use, I yelled to the man to call off his dog. For months afterwards, I had a purple weal the size of a half-crown. Lesson: never let an unfriendly sheepdog get behind you.

The road and railway from Mallaig go south hand in hand along the coast to Keppoch, famed for its glorious seascapes, and Arisaig, a small village beloved of discerning holidaymakers who find there tranquillity in alliance with an enchanting coast. Then both lines of communication aim due east along the southern boundary of Morar, passing Loch nan Uamh where Bonnie Prince Charlie landed from France in 1745 to conduct an abortive crusade that ended in defeat at Culloden.

Looking towards the head of Loch Morar

The tourist-ridden and sophisticated coast of Morar is not representative of the district. The true heart of Morar is in its unfrequented interior where tourists never go and only the brave venture.

There is a narrow road from the coast along the north side of Loch Morar as far as the little settlement of Bracorina and, from here, an easy climb to the crest of the ridge behind reveals a superlative view of Loch Nevis and Loch Morar, which are now little more than a mile apart. From this vantage point, the heads of both lochs are seen to be terminated by a group of mountains that seem to bar further progress eastwards. These mountains stand on a watershed between east and west and determined walkers blessed with unfailing energy will find a way from one side to the other much easier than is apparent on the approach.

From the end of the road at Bracorina, a track continues along the lochside to South Tarbet Bay where it crosses a narrow isthmus to Tarbet on Loch Nevis. From South Tarbet, the walk onwards to the head of Loch Morar along the north shore is a very rough five miles and for tough guys only. On arriving, one will see there are two possible ways through the mountains, the easier being that to the south where a main feeder of the loch can be followed up to the watershed. Here it becomes clear that this route from Morar is in fact a simple passage to a valley draining east to less harsh landscapes ahead.

Morar is left behind at the watershed and the district of Lochaber entered.

The Fort William to Mallaig line, near Arisaig

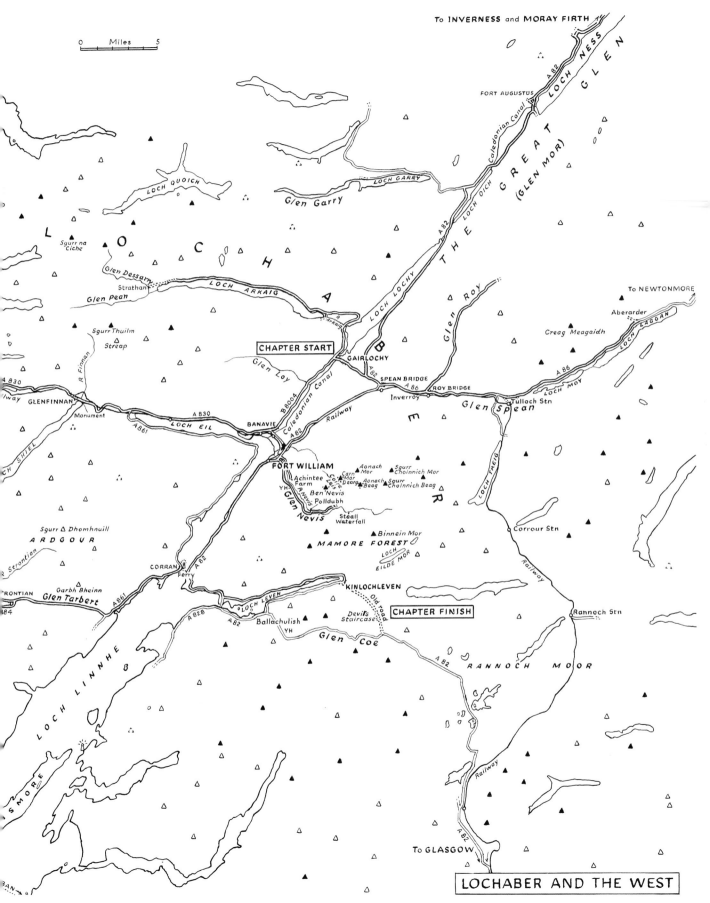

LOCHABER AND THE WEST

LOCHABER AND THE WEST

THERE IS a geological rift, a channel of low ground, between the Great Glen and the west coast occupied by Loch Arkaig and Loch Morar, the eight miles from one to the other being an easily negotiable pedestrian pass. High mountains in the middle section define the watershed, streams draining west from it to Morar and east to Lochaber but all are destined for the Atlantic.

There was talk some time ago of constructing a motor road through the pass, extending the present road alongside Loch Arkaig through Glen Pean and over the pass. Such a road would be a scenic delight and give an alternative road to the Isles but it has not yet happened and, it is to be hoped, never will. A highway along the side of Loch Morar would destroy the solitude. And solitudes are precious and becoming more so. The silence of the wild places should be disturbed only by the sounds of nature. Man is an unwelcome intruder.

UPPER LOCHABER

This part of Lochaber is invariably entered from Gairlochy by the only road leading into the interior of the district: a narrow switchback strip of tarmac alongside the twelve-mile length of Loch Arkaig to its end at the solitary croft of Strathan, encompassed by lofty heights, many of them of Munro status. Here, faced by uncompromising contours, the glen branches into two, Glen Pean and Glen Dessarry, either of which can be followed on foot to Loch Morar: a long and arduous trek.

Loch Arkaig

The mountains south of the head of Loch Arkaig are fully in view from the end of the road, Sgurr Thuilm and Streap in particular being well displayed, but to see the even grander mountains bordering Glen Dessarry, a short walk up this glen should be taken. Here, in grim surroundings, ride the satellite peaks of Sgurr na Ciche, most graceful of all.

This is a lonely and inhospitable region of rough sheep pastures, tamed only by the public road and the scraping of the earth around a few isolated crofts.

Gairlochy

The north shore of Loch Arkaig rises steadily to an indistinct range of high country beyond which is Glen Garry; this range ends abruptly in the east where steep slopes descend to Loch Lochy in the Great Glen. South of Loch Arkaig and east of its high fringe of Munros is a broad tract of undulating moorlands dissected by lonely glens and watercourses draining into Loch Eil, familiar to users of the Mallaig road and railway. The eastern boundary is the Great Glen.

The eastern end of Loch Arkaig, in complete contrast to its middle and upper reaches, is beautifully wooded. Issuing from the loch is the River Arkaig, crossing a narrow strip of land and less than a mile in length before entering Loch Lochy. The road also crosses this green strath turning south to reach the attractive village of Gairlochy, continuing as a quiet country road to Banavie, with an abandoned railway and the River Lochy in close company. From it, Glen Loy opens an inviting way into the hilly interior but the object that most excites attention is the tremendous bulk of Ben Nevis on the far side of the valley, better seen from here than from any other low viewpoint.

Ben Nevis

Glenfinnan

ARDNAMURCHAN AND ARDGOUR

I have less to say about the country south of the Mallaig railway. I have travelled the region many times and always with enjoyment, but never with the eager anticipation of journeys in the north. Here we have left the Highlands behind and there is not even a single Munro to look at and admire.

The landscapes are pleasantly rural and in places beautiful, but they lack excitement; it is a district where dairy cows and fat sheep are more likely to be seen than eagles and deer, and gentle streams rather than mountain cataracts. My preoccupation with the scenery of the Highlands and the western fiords leads me to feel that I should really be elsewhere, say in Glen Nevis or Torridon. A landscape without a mountain background is for me incomplete.

However I must sink my prejudices and draw attention to those places that have given me special pleasure.

The area can be reached from a junction on the Mallaig road at Loch Ailort on a delightful coastal journey with glorious views seawards and lovely sandy beaches, then crossing the Moidart peninsula to arrive at the village of Acharacle. Visitors unencumbered by cars get an even better introduction by embarking at Glenfinnan on the small passenger boat that plies the seventeen miles of Loch Shiel and delivers them at Acharacle without effort on their part: an idyllic cruise.

The most popular halting place on the Mallaig road occurs midway along it at the village of Glenfinnan where romance is allied to scenic beauty of a high order. Even the railway has charm as it curves on a fine viaduct where the River Finnan comes down from the mountains to enter Loch Shiel, a long and narrow sheet of water passing through high portals to reach green pastures after a serpentine course of seventeen miles. All visitors to Glenfinnan visit the prominent monument near the head of the loch, erected in 1815 to commemorate the Highlanders who rallied to the cause of Prince Charlie in 1745.

From Acharacle, the A.861 climbs over a low ridge to Salen, a village on the shore of Loch Sunart, reaching it through a pleasant woodland and between ditches of yellow flag iris. There is an agreeable atmosphere of rural tranquillity here; the environment is charming, as is the friendly village.

At Salen, the road forks and a decision must be taken: whether to go on the B.8007 to Ardnamurchan Point, a twenty-six-mile journey (and twenty-six back): this is the most westerly point of the Scottish mainland and, for this reason, attracts many tourists; or to continue along the A.861 to the Corran Ferry and Fort William.

The answer depends on the weather. On a bright clear day it must be Yes to Ardnamurchan Point; on a wet and misty day, it must certainly be No.

Loch Sunart

Ardnamurchan Point

ARDNAMURCHAN

Ardnamurchan is a long peninsula thrusting far into the Atlantic, having a coastline fretted with bays and coves and a hilly hinterland uncultivated except for a scattering of crofts. The B.8007 from Salen runs the full length of the peninsula, keeping close to the southern shore and serving the little settlements of Borrodale, Mingary and Kilchoan.

The road from Salen is the tenuous lifeline of Ardnamurchan, the vital link with the world outside its boundaries. It is narrow with passing places; it winds in and out and up and down to circumvent natural obstacles, and progress is slow by main road standards. The scenery alongside is mostly dull and uninteresting with occasional vistas worth capturing by the camera, the rocky and indented coast contributing greatly.

At Glen Borrodale, a tropical oasis, are massed banks of rhododendrons by the roadside and a cluster of offshore islands, making a captivating picture. Further, confronted by the uncompromising Ben Hiant (the Holy Mountain) which, rising to 1729 feet, bars the way forward, the road turns inland for several miles into a bare moorland before the contours relent and permit a return to the coast. Next of interest is the ruined Mingary Castle, a thirteenth-century stronghold dramatically sited on the brink of sea cliffs; from a nearby pier, there is a once-daily passenger ferry to Tobermory on the island of Mull. The next inhabited place is Kilchoan, the principal village on the peninsula, and six miles beyond, across a featureless moor, the lighthouse on Ardnamurchan Point is reached in a surround of naked rock and low cliffs. The keeper of the lighthouse is permitted to admit visitors. The views seaward are unrivalled anywhere. From the vast expanse of water many islands are seen: Rum, Eigg and Muck in the north, Coll and Tiree in the west, with a distant profile of Barra and Uist in the Outer Hebrides and, much nearer, Mull closes the southern horizon.

This is truly land's end. This is not only the most westerly point of the mainland of Scotland but of Britain also, being further west than the better known Land's End in Cornwall and incomparably finer, quite unspoilt and free of tourist invasions and commercial enterprises.

Ardnamurchan Point, on a fine day, more than justifies the long and tortuous journey necessary to see its beautiful seascapes, the best of all.

The other road out of Salen is the continuation of the A.861, heading eastwards along the shore of Loch Sunart, which here forms the southern boundary of the district of Ardgour, another tract of high ground cut into by long glens. There are extensive conifer plantations and a nature reserve. The other boundaries are Loch Shiel in the west, Loch Eil in the north and Loch Linnhe in the east. It is not a tourist area, having only a sparse and scattered population, but is deserving of attention by searchers after peace and seclusion.

After passing the shapely peak of Ben Resipol, the road reaches a fertile side valley occupied by the village of Strontian.

STRONTIAN

On a first visit, Strontian is a surprise, an anachronism. Here are not the terraces of single-storey cottages common to most Highland villages but dignified residences more akin to the suburbs of a large town. There is an air of prosperity, faded somewhat since the closing of the lead mines that contributed wealth to the community after the discovery of the metallic element strontium. The upper glen is delightful, the River Strontian and lovely trees giving it a parklike character. You can see here the abrupt double peak of Sgurr Dhomhnuill.

Beyond Strontian, Loch Sunart comes to an end and the A.884, a narrow road, branches from the A.861 to round the head of the loch, travel along its southern shore for some miles and then cross the moorlands of Morvern to its terminus at Lochaline, a small coastal village with castle ruins nearby and a seasonal car ferry to the island of Mull.

Morvern is a peninsula and almost an island, having sea water on all sides and a connection with the mainland only to the east of Loch Sunart. At Lochaline, the mainland ends.

Back on the A.861, the road goes forward along Glen Tarbert, passing Ardgour's greatest peak, Garbh Bheinn, a rockclimbers' favourite: its skyline, when seen from Loch Leven, resembles a prostrate Queen Victoria, bonnet and all. Then the great waterway of Loch Linnhe appears ahead and the road turns alongside Corran where, at the loch's narrowest part, a car ferry operates to the far bank, linking with the busy A.82 south of Fort William.

Corran ferry

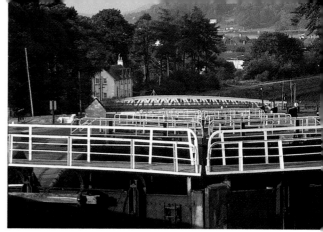

Urquhart Castle overlooking Loch Ness   *Neptune's Staircase*

THE GREAT GLEN

The Great Glen, as Glen Mor is commonly called, is the most remarkable physical feature of the Highlands. It is a geological fault, the result of a convulsion of nature in ages past when the north and north-west of Scotland moved away from the rest of the country, leaving a clear divide, straight as an arrow and sliced as though by a giant cleaver, across the breadth of Scotland from the Atlantic to the North Sea. Had the cut been only fifty feet deeper, it would have filled with sea water and the land to the north would have been an island. This long low channel through the mountains is occupied by three inland lochs: Loch Lochy, Loch Oich and Loch Ness, the latter made famous by people who think they have seen a monster in its waters. At one end, Loch Linnhe brings the Atlantic to the entrance to the glen; at the other end, the Moray Firth admits the North Sea.

The glen was an obvious subject for a canal that would obviate the necessity for small vessels to make the long and hazardous voyage around Cape Wrath and the northern coast, and in 1803 Thomas Telford was commissioned to construct a waterway to link the three lochs and connect with Loch Linnhe and the Moray Firth, thus giving a continuous water surface from the Atlantic to the North Sea. Of the sixty-mile length of the glen, two-thirds was already covered by the three lochs, these being of sufficient depth to permit the passage of small ships, and to join them together with access from Loch Linnhe and the Moray Firth, twenty-two miles of cuttings were needed, together with a system of locks to raise the canal from sea level to the slightly higher level of the glen at both ends with more at Fort Augustus. The series at Banavie at the Loch Linnhe end became known as 'Neptune's Staircase'.

The Caledonian Canal, as it was named, was an immediate success but its use declined with the coming of railways and faster forms of transport. It is still operational, and to see a ship gliding through fields and woodlands between steep mountain slopes can be quite startling. Today, it is mainly used by pleasure craft.

The Great Glen not only divides Scotland into two. It divides this book into two also. It marks the halfway stage in the itinerary and the halfway stage in the narrative. This is the place to close the book and go to bed. I am writing these lines on the last day of 1986, the deadline I set myself for reaching the Great Glen with my pen. So far we are on schedule. We all deserve a rest day, and conveniently at the halfway stage is Fort William, the only town in the itinerary thus far, where refuelling and restocking can take place for the second part of the journey.

NETHER LOCHABER

This is the best known part of Lochaber and indeed probably the best known part of the Highlands, familiar to most visitors to Scotland, featured in ballads and too often in newspaper headlines, a Mecca for adventurers and everywhere displaying spectacular scenery on a grand scale.

FORT WILLIAM

And so we arrive at Fort William. Not by the route the signposts have been urging ever since faraway Loch Carron but by way of Corran Ferry after a protracted series of diversions and deviations.

Two miles of hotels, guest houses and even motels, all facing Loch Linnhe, line the road into the town. This road, the A.82, once served as the main shopping street but has recently been re-routed to avoid congestion. Few touring visitors wish to bypass the shops, however, using the large car parks and walking around the streets. This is the principal shopping centre in the west of Scotland north of Glasgow, and the supplier of needs within a fifty-mile radius. The main street is usually very crowded.

Nothing remains of the original fort, built in 1655 by General Monk to repel Jacobite invaders, but relics of these troubled times can be seen in the public museum.

The town is situated on the shore of Loch Linnhe at the entrance to the Great Glen and has a harbour to accommodate commercial vessels and pleasure boats in an unattractive waterfront. The railway comes into the town from Glasgow after a circuitous journey across Rannoch Moor, and a branch line departs for Mallaig. Motorists who are having a rest day at Fort William can be strongly recommended to travel to Mallaig and back on the train, getting a window seat and, for a change, feasting their gaze on the passing scenery and not on the road in front: an effortless journey of sheer delight all the way. The railway station has been re-sited down the line to make room for the town's bypass. The A.82 continues to Inverness along the Great Glen, accompanied as far as Fort Augustus by a disused railway track from Spean Bridge.

Tourism is the main industry and is thriving. A vast factory for paper-making was built nearby a few decades ago, becoming the town's main employer, but its future appears to be under threat. There are the inevitable distilleries: an industry that goes on for ever.

Fort William's greatest attraction is the huge mountain that dominates Lochaber and rises immediately behind the town, the highest mountain in Britain. Many people come to make the ascent, some to climb its tremendous cliffs, others merely to look at it. Ben Nevis is a huge magnet.

The main street in Fort William

Ben Nevis from Corpach

BEN NEVIS

Ben Nevis is not the killer mountain it is often represented to be in the popular press. Accidents do occur, and too frequently, usually to climbers on its dangerous cliffs, but these are due to human frailty and misjudgments, not to venomous attacks by the Ben. Indeed, it is a friendly giant, accepting geriatrics and infants with open arms, but it demands to be treated with respect and should never be under-estimated. The summit is 4406 feet higher than Loch Linnhe, and because its roots are at sea level and there are no possible elevated lift-offs from cars, the full height must be climbed on foot.

A much trodden tourist path leaves Achintee Farm in Glen Nevis and slants upwards to a midway plateau of open ground where the superstructure of the mountain towers. Here the path defeats the contours by zigzagging up to a final easy incline along the edge of cliffs to the Ordnance Survey column among the ruins of a former observatory. The path is unmistakable except in deep snow, when it should not be attempted, and has no difficulties other than unremitting steepness.

The tourist path, although free from hazards, is a weary treadmill, and active and experienced walkers can reserve it for a quick descent and adopt an alternative route by crossing the midway plateau and descending into the stony recesses of the Allt a' Mhuillinn by rounding the base of Castle Buttress. Walking upstream, the finest aspect of Ben Nevis is revealed: an intimidating succession of cliffs and rock buttresses 2000 feet high and riven by fearful gullies and palpably the preserve of expert cragsmen only. The valley of the Allt a' Mhuillinn can be followed to its head in Coire Leis and the ridge linking Carn Mor Dearg gained, this then being climbed to the summit. This is by far the most exciting way to the top, without danger and well within the powers of a strong walker. The tourist path then gives an exhilarating descent.

The view from the summit is far reaching, extending over half of Scotland and a confused jumble of a hundred peaks to the islands of the Hebrides.

I cannot recall seeing any other walkers when I climbed the Ben by the route I have described some thirty-odd years ago although the day was fine and the month May. This could not possibly happen today, when the tourist path is the scene of processions of aspiring and perspiring walkers with many fallen by the wayside. Ben Nevis is seldom lonely these days.

Above left and right *The summit of Ben Nevis*

Below *Looking south-east from the summit*

The Ben Nevis range from the Commando Memorial

THE BEN NEVIS RANGE

Ben Nevis stands at one end of the greatest mountain range in the Highlands, buttressing a grand array of ten Munros with altitudes above or near 4000 feet and forming an unbroken high skyline for several miles. The nearest neighbours of Ben Nevis, Carn Mor Dearg and Aonach Beag, both have summits above the 4000 mark; to another of the group, Aonach Mor, the Ordnance Survey rather churlishly ascribes a height of 3999 only, a tribute to their meticulous accuracy but a pity they could not have permitted themselves a slight error of twelve inches. The high ground continues eastwards, the twin Sgurr Choinnichs being next in line; this is followed by an upland area known as the Grey Corries, so called because of the pallid appearance of the scree-covered upper slopes and summits of the peaks above. The only breach in the mountain barrier occurs here, a low pass carrying a track from Glen Spean to the head of Loch Treig. Then there is a final upthrust of Munros before the range ends abruptly in a steep decline to Loch Treig.

Most of these mountains can be seen on a walk to the watershed of Glen Nevis, but foreshortening robs them of distinctive summits. Their appearance is that of an indefinite mountain wall, incredibly high, and does not invite ascent. From Glen Spean in the north, however, the full range is splendidly in view, the distance of a few miles revealing the individual summits in true perspective.

These mountains are attractive when seen from a distance, their summits neatly carved and the connecting ridges gracefully curved, but they lose their allure on close acquaintance. With the exceptions of Ben Nevis and Carn Mor Dearg, they are seldom visited, can only be approached from distant bases in the north, are difficult of access, progress being impeded by new conifer plantations, have no guiding paths to their summits and are unkind underfoot. They should be left to the collectors of Munros. They are not for genteel walkers.

GLEN SPEAN

The A.82 road from Fort William to Spean Bridge, although affording glimpses of Ben Nevis and company, and introducing a vast cattle ranch on a Wild West scale, is too busy for leisurely contemplation of the scenery. At Spean Bridge, however, it turns sharply uphill to the Commando Memorial and then descends to follow the Great Glen to Inverness. Continuing east from Spean Bridge along Glen Spean is the A.86, bound for Newtonmore in the Spey valley, and this, in comparison, is relatively quiet and passes through a succession of lovely scenes and interesting features. Spean Bridge and Roy Bridge, two miles further, are excellent centres for exploring this beautiful valley; there are charming riverside rambles and enjoyable walks in the foothills, and both villages have the advantage of railway stations. With the help of the train, a good expedition is available for hardy walkers: a path leaving Inverroy goes south through a low pass through the mountains to the head of Loch Treig, from which Corrour's lonely railway station may be reached; or, better still, done in reverse by taking the morning train to Corrour. Similarly using the train, and with less effort, the glen may be followed up-river to the station at Tulloch.

The railway in Glen Spean is the popular West Highland line between Glasgow and Fort William, a triumph of railway engineering through difficult terrain and completed only after incredible hardships and repeated problems in laying the line across the bogs of the desolate Moor of Rannoch.

Fort William is due north of Glasgow but the Ben Nevis range effectively barred a direct course for the line. The only possible way was to the north-east and east along Glen Spean where a level contour could be maintained for nearly twenty miles until, at Tulloch, the first opportunity of circumventing the mountain barrier was presented by the deep trench of Loch Treig to the south and reached by a steep gradient. An easier rise beyond the loch led to Corrour and the wilderness of Rannoch Moor.

This railway has given me much pleasure. It is always a thrilling experience to make the journey with face pressed against the carriage window. This is the most interesting of all British railways, passing through extremes of scenery. It is well patronised and not under threat of closure. It must be preserved.

Spean Bridge

Glen Roy

GLEN ROY

From Roy Bridge, a narrow road leads north into Glen Roy. Almost without exception, the visitors who turn up this road do so having heard or read of the 'parallel roads', a remarkable geological antiquity found in other Scottish glens but nowhere as clearly defined as in Glen Roy. The so-called roads, three in number, are scars visible around the valley, each maintaining a level contour and therefore obviously formed by water. They are, in fact, the beaches of ice-drained lakes left behind by successive falls in the glacier as it melted and was released from the valley at the end of the Ice Age. The motor road reaches a car park and viewpoint from which this phenomenon can be observed.

Historic cairns in Glen Spean

Creag Meagaidh

The A.86, widened and improved, turns north-east at Tulloch and for ten miles has the waters of Loch Moy and Loch Laggan alongside, ultimately arriving in the Spey valley. This is a useful cross-country route, pleasant but unexciting. Its best feature is Creag Meagaidh, 3700 feet, with a nature reserve on its lower slopes; unfortunately, this giant is out of sight from the road but is seen well after a short climb on a path from Aberarder Farm, worth doing for a view of the craggy east face of the mountain.

The dam on Loch Moy

GLEN NEVIS

Every sojourner in Fort William simply must pay a visit to Glen Nevis, even giving preference to it over the train journey to Mallaig if time is limited. There is a road along the glen to its head and, although the sight and sound of motor cars in places of quiet beauty is always a disturbing distraction, the road in Glen Nevis must be accepted because it gives an opportunity to inactive or disabled visitors to see the natural wonders and splendours of this spectacular defile between high mountain ranges. Everyone should see Glen Nevis. Every step of the way, every turn of the wheels, reveals fresh delights.

It caters for all tastes. There are quiet riverside nooks for meditation, wild flowers in the meadows and woodland glades, subjects galore for the artist and photographer, entrancing paths for the walker and a fine array of a score of challenging peaks for the mountaineer. There are waterfalls and cascades, cliffs and rocks, native trees and rampant heather in an earthly paradise.

The glen is threaded by the River Nevis, rather sedate in maturity but dancing with fun and high spirits in infancy. It is born in the upper reaches of the glen, and its godfathers are a group of lofty peaks beyond the haunts of tourists. It is augmented by tributaries and the magnificent waterfall of Steall and then plunges down a rocky wooded gorge, finally to travel on a more tranquil course to its destiny in Loch Linnhe.

But it is the enclosing mountains that are the most impressive and arresting features of the glen. On the north side is the massive wall of Ben Nevis and neighbouring heights; on the south side are the shapely peaks of Mamore Forest, every one strongly individual in character. If a walk is taken into the higher fastnesses of the glen, as may quite easily be done for several miles, more and more appear in succession; indeed, there is a through route for walkers, not available to those who have to return to parked cars, all the way to Loch Treig and Corrour Station: a memorable expedition.

The road along the glen is a leafy avenue for four miles to Polldubh, rising hardly at all in this distance but, after crossing the river over an exuberant cascade, climbs steadily for two more miles to a large car park at its terminus, passing a long waterslide coming down from Ben Nevis, which is unseen but directly above and 4000 feet higher. From the car park, a path goes forward, turning along the side of an immense gorge, roughly picking a way between trees of pine and birch with the river rushing madly below in a chaos of fallen rocks and boulders: this is a tremendous scene. Then, suddenly and unexpectedly, the path emerges from the gloom of the gorge into an open amphitheatre, a green strath as pleasant as a meadow, the river now meandering gently across it. All around are rough mountain slopes and, directly ahead, coming off the Mamores, the graceful plunge of Steall Waterfall, 350 feet high. Most visitors go no further although the path continues quite easily up-river.

Other people, some obviously unused to rough walking and ill-equipped for it, will inevitably be encountered on the popular path through the gorge, their approach being heralded by screams and shouts, to the dismay of those who prefer to be solitary and silent amidst scenes of grandeur, but this is a place where the company of others must be accepted with good grace. It is less easy to forgive the carriers of blaring transistor radios, a sacrilege in such surroundings.

I consider Glen Nevis to be the finest of Scottish glens.

Opposite, left to right *Polldubh waterfall; path through the gorge; Steall waterfall*

Above *Glen Nevis*

Kinlochleven and Mamore Forest

MAMORE FOREST

Mamore Forest is not a forest of trees but a bare upland formed into a series of individual peaks, every one of distinctive outline and separate from its fellows, every one inviting ascent. They stand in a line along the south side of Glen Nevis, worthy counterparts to those of the Ben Nevis range on the north side, not quite as high but of better appearance and much more photogenic from the floor of the glen.

And here too, are ten Munros, lending themselves admirably to a complete traverse from end to end in one of the finest of all mountain expeditions but one needing the expertise of experience. Novices should be content with one per day. The highest peak is Binnein Mor, 3700 feet.

Bounded by Glen Nevis on the north, the southern boundary of the Mamores is even better defined by Loch Leven and Loch Eilde Mor, to which their slopes descend steeply and roughly. At the head of Loch Leven is the small town of Kinlochleven, a very convenient base for their exploration.

KINLOCHLEVEN

Prior to the closing of the Ballachulish ferry and its replacement by a bridge, Kinlochleven was on the main A.82 and a popular place of call for motorists. The sixteen-mile detour around Loch Leven was much preferred to a long wait at the ferry, and the journey was made palatable by the excellence of the scenery and the opportunity of shopping or refreshment.

Although having a population of less than a thousand, public street lighting, bus depots and council housing estates give the town an urban character and its isolated situation at the head of the loch adds a feeling of insularity.

Kinlochleven must be classed as an industrial community because of the aluminium works, a vast complex that provides the main source of employment and was the cause of its emancipation from a village.

Despite the dominant aluminium works, the setting of Kinlochleven in a mountain surround is very pleasing and, apart from expeditions to the high places, there are splendid walks to be enjoyed.

Leaving the town on the south side is the Devil's Staircase, a military road constructed at the time of the Jacobite rebellion, and not at all as fearsome as the name implies. It leads unerringly over an intervening ridge and descends to the A.82 at the head of Glen Coe, providing excellent views throughout. The military road also connected with Fort William and offers walkers a splendid route at a high level but skirting the mountains, greatly to be preferred to the bus service.

For a short stroll, the path to Loch Eilde Mor can be climbed for a mile to get a perfect full-length view of Loch Leven.

Kinlochleven

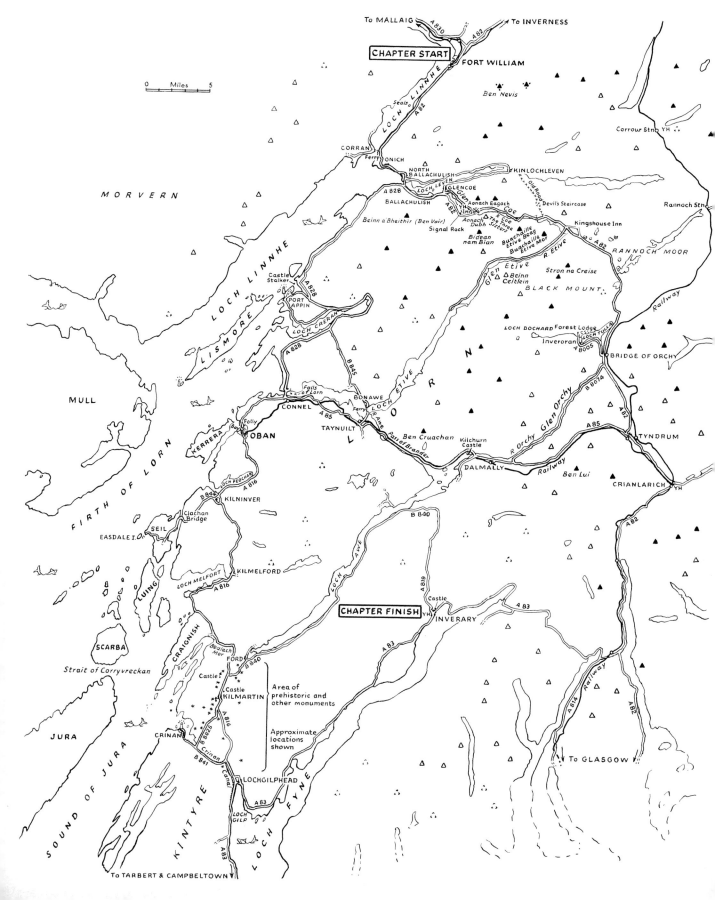

ARGYLL

RESUMING THE itinerary, Fort William is left by the southbound A.82, closely following the shore of Loch Linnhe. This is a busy road, being not only the route to Glasgow but having branches to other centres of population along the way.

Beyond the built-up area, a wide valley opens on the left and reveals a last sighting of Ben Nevis, as majestic as ever. Further, a hundred yards off-shore but masked by roadside trees, is a small islet often occupied by seals. Then Corran Ferry is reached.

I was once travelling by bus from Kinlochleven to Fort William, and was the only passenger, when the bus made its customary halt at Corran Ferry. Suddenly the conductress, hitherto placid and uncommunicative, erupted in a frenzy of excitement, pointing out to me a man standing at the water's edge: it was Peter Finch, she told me, here for the making of a film of Robert Louis Stevenson's *Kidnapped*. He was dressed for his role, his hair in a small pigtail. This disclosure made little impact on me, to her obvious disappointment, but left her atremble for the rest of the journey.

Beyond Corran Ferry, the road passes through the straggling village of Onich, pleasantly residential with hotels, guest houses and caravan parks for visitors who prefer its quiet environment to the bustle of Fort William; its situation at the point where Loch Leven turns inland from Loch Linnhe is blessed with fine views across the water. Next is North Ballachulish, where the road to Kinlochleven branches off, and ahead is the modern bridge over Loch Leven. This replaces the ferry that was such a help and yet such an obstacle to progress, queues of vehicles being halted at both sides, reconciled to lengthy waits. Today there is no slackening of speed across the bridge, denying the opportunity to inspect the glorious prospect up the loch to the mountains of Glen Coe, a scene that formerly regaled the passengers in waiting cars.

Glencoe from Loch Leven

From the north side of the Ballachulish bridge, and looking across the loch, a splendid group of mountains is seen to form a striking skyline above wooded foothills. The highest of the group is Beinn a' Bheithir, more often and more easily referred to as Ben Vair. The complete traverse of the skyline, in plan a horseshoe, makes an excellent day-long expedition, but not one to be undertaken lightly.

The summit of Ben Vair now has the distinction of forming part of the new regional boundary, the local government authorities obviously preferring a watershed boundary to the former valley divide provided by Loch Leven. Thus all streams draining into Loch Leven and Glen Coe are now in the Highland Region and those flowing south are in Strathclyde.

The long deep furrow occupied by Loch Leven formed an obvious boundary between the counties of Inverness and Argyll until the local government reorganisation in 1974; since then, incongruously, this natural boundary has been discarded in favour of an arbitrary line some miles south, dividing the Highland Region and, again incongruously, not Argyll but Strathclyde. Argyll has now vanished from the county map, but not from the hearts and minds of those who live in this beautiful area. To them, and many others, Argyll will always be Argyll.

At the end of the bridge, the roads have been improved with elegant overhead lighting and partly re-routed. There is a choice: left on the A.82 for Glasgow via Glen Coe, right for Oban via Appin. Appin is *Kidnapped* country and on a small hill near the junction is a memorial to James Stewart, who was wrongfully hanged for the murder of Colin Campbell, the Red Fox of the story.

Most wheels turn along the A.82. Earlier fleeting glimpses of the magnetic surroundings of Glen Coe make the choice an easy one for travelling tourists. Ballachulish village is passed, and the gigantic spoil-heaps by the roadside tell of earlier times when the quarrying of roofing slates was a booming industry here. Then the road from Kinlochleven joins in and the portals of Glen Coe are entered.

GLEN COE

Glen Coe is high drama. The scenery is tremendously impressive. It is the best known of all the Scottish glens – famous for its tragic history, an international reputation as a climbing ground where mountaineers and cragsmen can test their skills but, especially when under snow, dangerous for lesser fry and providing an emotional experience for all who come this way. The glen is a deep cutting between intimidating mountains: one side is formed by a serrated ridge difficult to attain and more difficult to traverse; on the other side are three savage and near-vertical buttresses of daunting aspect. These are known as the Three Sisters of Glen Coe, strangely because there is certainly nothing feminine about them; they are brutally masculine, threatening and, when wreathed in swirling mist, even frightening. Glen Coe is no place for the timid.

Two roads lead into Glen Coe from the west. The A.82 is a fast double-track road, but greatly to be preferred is the old road. It leaves the main road at a tangent and initially forms the main street of Glencoe village, previously known as Carnoch, which is lined with cottages to the old bridge over the River Coe, a picturesque spot. Nearby and reached by a two-minute walk is a monument dedicated to MacIan, chief of the Macdonald clan in Glen Coe, who perished with many of his people in the 1692 massacre. Over the bridge, the road continues as a delightful leafy and flowery avenue for two miles to the Clachaig Inn where, clear of trees, the might and majesty of the enclosing heights are fully appreciated.

Ballachulish Bridge

Opposite the inn, the hillside is cleft from top to bottom by a deep ravine, the Clachaig Gully, which in its gloomy depths gives continuous rockclimbing through a height of 1700 feet, the longest gully climb in Scotland and exclusively for experts only. The ridge above, continuing east and forming the northern boundary of the glen, is Aonach Eagach, also calling for skill and experience in negotiating its rocky pinnacles: the complete traverse of the ridge is an adventure long remembered. On the south side of the glen, and directly facing, is Aonach Dubh, buttressing and hiding rising ground behind that culminates in the summit of Bidean nam Bian, at 3766 feet the dominant height of Glen Coe.

From the Clachaig Inn, a short walk across to the main road and then a path leads to the Signal Rock, a bare mound in the midst of trees from which the Macdonald clan, who lived in Glen Coe, were summoned in times of crisis.

But it is the roadside field immediately beyond the inn, indicated by a noticeboard, that halts all travellers: this was the scene of the treacherous attack on the Macdonalds by the Campbells in alliance with Government troops, resulting in the annihilation of Macdonalds. The year was 1692 and although three hundred years have passed, the event still provokes bitter memories. It is a sad place. Glen Coe, in Gaelic, is interpreted as the Glen of Weeping: a name singularly appropriate.

Glen Coe, near the site of the massacre

Loch Achtriochtan in Glen Coe

Beyond the site of the massacre, the old road joins the new for the long climb through the glen. Travellers on foot, from here onwards to the head of the glen, can avoid the tarmac and the traffic, by persisting along the old road which has now degenerated into a grass track through neglect. It is generally easy to identify, except where the new road cuts across it, and an interesting exercise.

The journey up the glen, whether on wheels or on foot, is very impressive. Aonach Dubh is succeeded by its two rugged sisters; high on the former is Ossian's Cave, appearing like a giant keyhole in a wall of rock. It is thought to be named after a Gaelic poet of long ago. After the third buttress, the high barrier is broken by a steep-sided opening bringing a stream down from the unseen heights beyond. This gives access to walkers and is the usual route of ascent to Bidean nam Bian.

The roads, both old and new, now rise more sharply, the A.82 passing through a rock cutting and coming alongside an attractive waterslide where an enterprising piper often performs to an admiring audience, and reaching easier gradients as the top of the glen is approached. The old road here joins and is overlaid by the new.

The Three Sisters of Glen Coe

In a more open landscape, but still with lofty mountains alongside on the right, the A.82 now aims purposefully eastwards as though glad to escape the confines of the lower glen, straight miles taking over from tortuous curves. The ridge to the north becomes less imposing and, at a solitary roadside cottage, a signpost indicates a path up and over it to Kinlochleven: this is the old military road known as the Devil's Staircase (*see* p. 131). It is much less forbidding than the name suggests and well within the powers of the average walker.

It is the mountains to the south however, that arrest and compel attention: here they rise as individuals, not as part of a mass, and tower skywards in isolation, divided from each other by deep-sided glens. The first of these is Buachaille Etive Beag, soaring proudly from a peaty moor. The second and greater of the two is Buachaille Etive Mor, a pyramid of rock and scree, with an immensely strong personality and a summit palpably impossible of attainment by ordinary mortals without wings; however, the steep turrets and buttresses are beloved of rockclimbers, whose accounts of their ascents make thrilling reading.

I always look forward to a first glimpse of Buachaille Etive Mor when travelling north over Rannoch Moor. I think of it as the sentinel of Glen Coe, the harbinger of excitement soon to come. It is a mountain I can look at for hours but never with any thought of trying to climb it. I am content to let it remain one of my many Scottish virgins.

Buachaille Etive Mor

GLEN ETIVE

The two Buachailles were clearly given their names from Glen Etive, which extends south from them for several miles, and not from the moor to the north crossed by the A.82 from where they are most often seen.

Beyond Buachaille Etive Mor, a narrow side road leaves the A.82 for Glen Etive and although it comes to an end and the return must be made the same way, it is a deviation strongly recommended, well worth the extra miles, not only for the tranquil beauty of this little-visited valley but also for the surprising aspect of the two Buachailles when seen from the south.

The road runs in the company of the River Etive along the base of Buachaille Etive Mor, disclosing this mountain to be not the sharp cone it appeared to be from the A.82 but a three-mile ridge declining from the summit and becoming less formidable, offering walkers a scrambling route of ascent. On the east side of the glen is Sron na Creise, the first peak in a separate upland range known as the Black Mount (*see* p. 140). After four miles, the road curves west to avoid the steep upthrust of Beinn Ceitlein directly ahead and then enters the pleasant green strath of the glen. Resist the temptation to look back until two miles further, then do so and admire the perfect symmetry of the two Buachailles, the two Shepherds of Etive as they are affectionately named.

The road ends a mile further at a small pier at the head of Loch Etive, a ten-mile track continuing for walkers to Bonawe for Oban. On the far side of the loch, the peaks of the Black Mount stand in fine array. Glen Etive is very sparsely populated and there are no inducements other than the scenery to delay a return to the A.82.

Loch Etive

Rannoch Moor

The A.82 goes on, inclining south and bypassing the Kingshouse Inn, now promoted to Hotel, which the old road used to visit. When conditions are favourable for skiing, a chair-lift ascends the lower slopes of another of the Black Mount fraternity. Beyond this possible diversion, the Moor of Rannoch is entered.

RANNOCH MOOR

Rannoch Moor is a desolation fashioned by Nature and right well has she succeeded. A thousand feet above sea level and sixty square miles in extent, the moor is a vast tableland, so flat that it appears at first sight to be ideal terrain for walking. It is nothing of the sort, found on close acquaintance to be a labyrinth of bogs, pools, lochans and lochs, stagnant watercourses unable to decide which way to go, and squelching morasses. Through this unfriendly maze progress is possible only by repeated trials and errors. The Ordnance mapmakers must have torn out their hair by the roots when they came to survey and chart this frustrating wasteland: nothing remains constant for more than a few paces. Maps, lacking detail, promise an exhilarating tramp from the road to the railway stations at Corrour and Rannoch, many miles distant, and the few who know the moor well can enjoy threading a way between the obstacles; to everyone else, it is the stuff of which nightmares are made.

An excellent route for walkers, however, and no longer negotiable by vehicles, is provided by the old road which, from Kingshouse, skirts the west edge of the moor below the ramparts of the Black Mount and arrives after ten miles at Forest Lodge; from here, it continues as a tarmac road to Inveroran and Bridge of Orchy where the A.82 is rejoined. This old road, reduced in status to a footpath, is a joy that motorists cannot share. It is likely to be subject to an increase in foot traffic, however, having been incorporated in the new long-distance footpath, the West Highland Way, the finest of all pedestrian marathons.

I never tire of Rannoch Moor. It always gives me pleasure in any conditions, sunlit or under brooding cloud: the silence, the solitude, the panoramas of distant mountains etched against the sky in all directions, the resident deer, the heather, the bog myrtle, all contribute a charm to this no-man's-land. Here is desolation with a subtle beauty.

View from Forest Lodge

THE BLACK MOUNT

Rannoch Moor is ringed by mountains, some around the perimeter, others more distant, and a few on far horizons visible only in clear weather. The nearest in view is the range of the Black Mount, forming a rugged façade along the western edge of the moor, broken into corries but maintaining a high skyline throughout and rising to distinct peaks, many of them Munros. This range is seen to advantage from the A.82, better even than from the old road, which is too near the base of the range to yield a correct perspective. The range extends from Kingshouse to a sudden end at Forest Lodge, a ten-mile barrier without an easy passage through.

In addition to the summits seen from the A.82, there are others hidden behind, the hinterland being an unfrequented wilderness of mountains dissected by lonely glens, stretching west to Glen Etive without habitations or hospitality and only a remote chance of help if help is needed. It behoves all who venture beyond the fringe of this upland desert to have regard to the time of day and the distance from base. As with other mountain fastnesses in Scotland, care is needed in route selection, twice the expected time should be allowed for an expedition, and arctic clothing and food reserves should be carried.

The Black Mount is not for gentle ramblers.

The Black Mount from Forest Lodge

Although the Black Mount must be regarded by walkers of no more than average ability as strictly out of bounds, there is one route available to them for circumventing the high ground and gaining access to the interior of the mountain mass and surveying at close range peaks that are not visible from the main road. Moreover, this route is so easy, the use of it seems almost like cheating.

River Dochard

At Forest Lodge, accessible by cars along the old road from Bridge of Orchy, a cart track heads west along a side glen abounding in deer and, in three miles, reaches Loch Dochard where there is an uninterrupted view of the mountains rising from its far shore. The profound silence and absence of movement add to the impressiveness of the scene and induce an uneasy feeling in observers with imaginative minds that they are looking at a dead world.

There is no point in going further. The track continues as a path to the inhospitable east shore of Loch Etive, a marathon trek practicable only to really tough hikers carrying tents.

The Bridge of Orchy

Bridge of Orchy is the only port of call between Kingshouse and Tyndrum on the long crossing of Rannoch Moor. Here the old road and the new converge after taking divergent routes over the moor, and here the railway comes alongside after a circuitous journey from Fort William. There is a hotel and a filling station on the A.82 and a few dwellings, but the importance of this halting stage is emphasised by a railway station on the hillside nearby.

Visitors who wonder where the bridge is that gives its name to the place will find it by taking a short stroll down the side road from the hotel; it carries the old road across the River Orchy on its way from Loch Tulla to Loch Awe and is worth a photograph.

The A.82 continues south in less romantic surroundings, poetry becoming prose, to Tyndrum, a village catering for the needs of tourists and once boasting *two* railway stations (one an un-manned halt), and goes on to Crianlarich, an important road and rail junction. It is from Crianlarich that our itinerary moves eastwards and finally north to the Cairngorms, but first a tour of old Argyll must be made. Crianlarich will be visited later.

GLEN ORCHY

The point of departure from the A.82 occurs a short mile south of Bridge of Orchy where a side road branches to the west and leads into Glen Orchy, a quiet and unspoilt valley away from the noise of traffic, every one of its unfrequented ten miles a pleasure to travel. As a lively companion to the narrow road is the delightful River Orchy, a salmon river with fish-passes and sparkling waterfalls.

This byway joins the main road to Oban, the A.85, and enters Dalmally.

River Orchy

River Orchy at Dalmally

Dalmally is a large village with a railway station on the Oban line, situated in a pleasant open strath through which the River Orchy meanders on the last stage of its journey to join Loch Awe. The nearest mountains keep at a respectful distance but there is no ignoring the massive bulk of Ben Cruachan, 3689 feet, filling the western sky; eastwards is Ben Lui, 3708 feet. Dalmally lies between the two but is not shadowed by either. The A.85 heads west with the railway, skirting the shore of Loch Awe and crossing a watery plain that the engineers of the former road were unable to tackle, their route making a long incursion to avoid the problem. Prominent in the loch is the sad ruin of the fifteenth-century Kilchurn Castle.

Kilchurn Castle

Loch Awe

LOCH AWE

It is not the head of Loch Awe that is met from Dalmally as may be supposed having regard to the lie of the land or from a casual glance at a map. It is an elongated bay.

Loch Awe's behaviour is extraordinary and unorthodox. It is twenty-five miles long and very narrow, lying across Argyll like a serpent and, as is the case with all lochs draining mountain areas, its waters are destined for the sea and arrive there by the shortest route permitted by the lie of the land. Loch Awe conforms to this rule in a most eccentric manner. Looking at a map, it would seem to be a safe bet that the surplus waters of the loch would discharge directly into the Atlantic, only *three* miles away from the southern end, instead of which the flow is inland *towards* the mountains for twenty miles, finally escaping by squeezing through the narrow Pass of Brander and emerging as a river to enter Loch Etive. From here, it is carried as a passenger in alien waters a further ten miles to the sea. Thus the outflow of Loch Awe elects to travel forty miles to a destination only three miles distant. Later on, we will visit the southern end of the loch and see why.

The Pass of Brander

THE PASS OF BRANDER

The road and railway turn along the shore of Loch Awe into the Pass of Brander, a narrow defile at the foot of Ben Cruachan, where the loch gradually tapers to an end and becomes the River Awe. Here the North of Scotland Hydro-Electric Board, also realising, against the odds, that this is the foot of the loch and not the head, have deposited immense quantities of concrete into the water and fashioned from it a vast complex of tunnels, underwater chambers and offices, with a dam and even an electric lift to help salmon enter the loch from the issuing river: the whole is an amazing enterprise which the Board proudly invites the public to inspect. The best thing they have done for walkers is to construct a road up the hillside of Ben Cruachan, this serving as a high springboard for the ascent.

Without the softening effect of trees, the pass would be exceedingly wild. The steep flanks on either side, broken by cliffs, add an oppressive gloom to the scene. The road and railway, in places cut out of the living rock, proceed close as brothers to emerge with the river into pastoral loveliness as all descend to the village of Taynuilt. This is the district of Lorn.

From Taynuilt, an attractive detour into Appin to see the setting of Stevenson's *Kidnapped* was formerly possible by using the Bonawe Ferry across Loch Etive, but this privilege is now denied to travellers following the ferry's closure. To visit Appin today from this direction, it is necessary to continue along the road to Connel, there crossing the bridge on the A.828 and following this northwards. It is a rewarding detour.

Ahead of us now is Loch Creran, an inlet of the sea that encroaches some miles inland and makes necessary a five-mile detour around its head to reach places of interest on its north shore. The narrows of Loch Creran were formerly crossed by a railway, now defunct, the bridge remaining as a skeletal relic, but today's travellers have no easy option: the road must be followed all the way around the head of the loch to arrive on the far bank, shouting distance only having been earned by the long detour. The road to Ballachulish then leaves the lochside and travels overland. From it branches a road to Port Appin, the primary objective of this excursion, reaching it in four interesting miles close to the water's edge.

PORT APPIN

Coming from an industrial and urban background, it is always a matter of wonder to me that communities, denied modern comforts, can exist in perfect contentment in places so remote and difficult of access and often in hostile surroundings that they live in a little world of their own, insular, independent, seemingly unaffected by outside pressures and problems, seeing the same few faces and following the same routine day after day throughout a lifetime. No live football matches to watch, no cinemas, no bingo, no supermarkets, no outside interests, nothing . . . or is there a quality of life beneath the veneer of sophistication most of us strive to acquire? Are we going the wrong way?

Port Appin is such a place. It occupies the tip of a ragged peninsula, so fretted by bays and coves and inlets that water appears in every scene as on an island. The village faces the sea on which its livelihood largely depends: there is a good harbour able to accommodate ships and a passenger ferry operates to the northern end of the sheltering island of Lismore. Activity is centred on the seafront to the music of rolling waves and screaming gulls. The inhabitants are smiling and helpful. Perhaps it is they who have found the secret of good living. Perhaps they are not to be pitied, but envied. Perhaps Port Appin has a lesson for its curious visitors.

The harbour, Port Appin

Castle Stalker

The A.828 can be rejoined from the village by an alternative road and should be taken for a further two miles to see the romantic and historic Castle Stalker on a rocky islet just offshore and accessible only by boat. It is in the form of a square keep and dates from the thirteenth century. Poised on its little perch with the blue hills of Morvern in the background across the waters of Loch Linnhe, it cries out for the attention of cameras. It makes a beautiful picture.

Having visited Port Appin and photographed Castle Stalker, cars must be turned around and the A.828 followed towards Oban, the mountain scenery of Loch Creran being better viewed on the return journey. Beyond the Bonawe junction, the main road continues along the lochside and arrives at Connel.

The imposing cantilever bridge across Loch Etive at Connel, out of keeping with its rural setting and more appropriate to a city, was the second largest of its type in Europe at the time of construction. It spans the narrows of the loch and, until 1966, carried the Oban–Ballachulish railway and a toll road, the railway being defunct and the tolls abolished. It remains a monument to Victorian enterprise.

There is a peculiarity about Loch Etive here. Although a sea loch, its waters are a few feet above sea level, to which it drops in a series of cascades to merge into the open sea. This miniature cataract has the name of the Falls of Lorn, and those are visible only at low tide; at high tide they are submerged.

Connel Bridge

The Falls of Lorn

OBAN

On the south side of the bridge at Connel, the A.85 from Taynuilt is joined for the last few miles into Oban, the views seawards being sadly marred by extensive caravan sites. There is no longer any feeling of loneliness. Rural changes to urban. The road becomes busy and has pavements and street lighting; commercial establishments appear. There is no doubt that we are entering a town of some importance. Oban vies with Fort William as the principal shopping, business and residential community on the western seaboard north of the Clyde, and is better looking. Its pulsating heart is the harbour, always throbbing with activity: a haven for fishing boats and a calling place for large ships, a place to leave the mainland for cruises to the islands. Facing the harbour is the main shopping street and on a hill-side behind is a pleasant suburbia amongst trees, dominated by a huge circular structure like a coliseum: this is McCaig's Folly, built by a local banker and intended as a museum and art gallery and a permanent memorial to himself, but abandoned after the outer walls were completed. It is alien to its surroundings but has the single merit of commanding a fine view of the town below and Oban Bay beyond.

Oban is the best springboard for visiting the western islands and has many charming walks on the low hills around. It is the terminus of a railway from Glasgow, the first two miles of a curving incline being exciting and scenically very attractive with enchanting views.

The harbour, Oban

McCaig's Folly

My first visit to Oban was not a happy experience. It happened forty years ago but I remember it well. I was looking for overnight lodgings and was persuaded by a sign proclaiming The Oban Hotel to enter a black-painted building that looked evil but which, I thought, with a proud name like that must be all right inside. It was evil inside too. Ten paces along a dingy vestibule with a foul smell and paper peeling from the walls was enough to convince me that I had made a mistake and I turned to flee only to find my exit barred by the proprietor who had emerged from a room along the passage. He was unwashed and half drunk but, with an expansive smile, assured me that he had a nice bedroom overlooking the harbour, with clean sheets on the bed, and I allowed him to shepherd me upstairs to it. He could see I was uneasy but promised me a good breakfast and said he charged only one pound to be paid in advance. I paid and he left. The room was sparsely furnished but, as he said, the sheets were clean. The bathroom alongside was a mess. The bath was full of odds and ends, there was no hot water in the tap, the w.c. wouldn't flush: the place was filthy.

I went out into the fresh air, had a meal in a café and walked the streets until eleven o'clock, not wanting to go back. When I did, I opened a downstairs door hoping for a better bathroom. There were four Lascars playing cards around a table and the proprietor sprawled in a chair, now dead drunk, obviously having consumed the pound I had given him. I backed out and went up to my room, barricading the door, which had no lock, with a chair, and had a restless night, very apprehensive that I might have my throat cut. Nothing happened; there were no sinister footsteps outside my door and I was relieved, after hours of deathly silence, to see the light of dawn filtering into the room and the welcome resumption of movement and noise in the street beneath my window.

I waited until seven o'clock, looking at my maps, and then went downstairs. The proprietor appeared at my call; sober and sullen and never said a word when I told him I wanted to catch an early train. After a few minutes, he produced a plate of rancid bacon and eggs and a pot of tea, much of which I left in my eagerness to get out of the place. I went along to the station, boarded the waiting train and with half an hour to wait for its departure, did all I needed to do in the toilet including a wash and a shave – although a notice told me I really shouldn't be doing these things while the train was stationary. Then I settled into a seat for the journey to Glasgow.

Since those early days I have returned to Oban many times, always with eager anticipation. The town has become a sophisticated holiday resort with modern hotels and shops and leisure areas and caravan sites, the latter developments mercifully out of sight of the harbour precincts, which remain unchanged. Up on the hill, the skeleton of McCaig's Folly still overlooks with sightless eyes the animated activity below. McCaig at least got his permanent memorial.

THE ARGYLL COAST

Our journey continues south from Oban, the absence of mountains in the landscape being compensated for by a picturesque coastal strip with many bays, inlets and off-shore islands, and rich in natural woodlands. An added attraction for those whose minds dwell on the ancient past is the profusion of prehistoric remains that has led to this part of Argyll earning the name of the Cradle of Scotland.

The road leaving Oban is the A.816 and, after a hilly and winding passage, it runs alongside Loch Feochan and arrives at the village of Kilninver where the B.844 branches to the right, offering a recommended detour. This side road leads to Clachan Bridge, a single span over a narrow channel to the island of Seil, the only example of the mainland being connected to an island by a bridge. To add to the unique interest, the waters below the bridge are those of the Atlantic, giving it the alternative name of Atlantic Bridge and the only instance of a bridge across part of the ocean. (Actually, the narrow channel is properly but less romantically known as the Sound of Seil.) The bridge, built in 1792, is attributed to Telford.

After the bridge, a road crosses Seil to its west shore where there is a colony of cottages and immense slate quarries, all now abandoned but once employing hundreds of men in a major industry. Off-shore is the small island of Easdale, also having large derelict quarries, a small ferry linking the two.

Returning to Kilninver, the A.816 is resumed southwards, every mile beautiful as it turns inland along a glen to circumvent the headland of Kilbrandon. The next village reached is Kilmelford situated at the head of Loch Melfort, a large inlet of the sea. The road follows the south shore, turns inland again before rising steeply to the high pass of the Bealach Mor, the incline having superb views across the peninsula of Craignish to the myriad of islands in the Sound of Jura, in particular the larger Scarba and Jura with the Strait of Corryvreckan, famous for its whirlpools, between the two.

Easdale from Seil

View from Bealach Mor

Over the Bealach Mor, the road descends to Kilmartin but before entering this village, the B.840 turns off to the left for Loch Awe, reaching after two miles the hamlet of Ford, where anglers foregather for the fishing in the loch; the road forks here to serve both sides of the loch, which is now immediately ahead. Our reason for making this short detour is to solve the puzzle why the waters of the loch do not discharge directly into the sea at this point instead of electing to travel forty miles across country with precisely the same objective, escaping through the Pass of Brander to join Loch Etive and reach the open sea beyond Connel. The reason for this extraordinary behaviour is now resolved. This end of Loch Awe is ringed by low hills that do not admit a water passage; there is no issuing stream. This is the *head* of the loch, not the foot as maps suggest. This is the start of it, not the end.

The scenery here is so bewitchingly beautiful that there is a temptation to drive further along the side of the loch, and of course this may be done if time allows; indeed, by travelling along the eastern side of the loch, Inveraray on the route of our itinerary may be reached. But there are other sights to see before arriving at Inveraray and these are found by returning to the A.816 and first parking the car at Kilmartin, where archaeologists will suffer paroxysms of delight and even the most prosaic of visitors will have their imaginations fired by the many remaining evidences of prehistoric occupation.

KILMARTIN

The tiny village of Kilmartin and around about have a profusion of Bronze Age and other ancient relics and sufficient medieval remains to suggest that this pleasant countryside has been in continuous human occupation for thousands of years. In the village is a ruined sixteenth-century castle, scene of an attempted assassination, of which little has survived, and the main attraction is the graveyard of the church where, inside the entrance arch forming a war memorial, are two famous crosses: one, with only the shaft remaining, bears two remarkable carvings of Christ and is one of the best surviving examples of Celtic art. Also in the graveyard are many richly sculptured stones, some in Government care and others depicting knights in armour.

While the principal treasures of Kilmartin are in the graveyard and church, outside the village, within easy reach, are chambered cairns and cup-and-ring markings on groups of rocks that have been there since before the dawn of history. It seems reasonable to assume that the early settlers arrived over the sea, found this fertile coastal strath to their liking and made their homes here.

Above left *Kilmartin Castle*, right *sculptured gravestone ;* below left *standing stones*, right *Celtic cross*

There are other signs of human activity in ages long past on the way south to Crinan, with occasional sightings of castles built long ago, so that one arrives at Crinan on the B.8025, with a mind saturated with prehistory only to be immediately jolted back to the present upon finding there a canal serving as a marina for yachts and other pleasure craft in a scene of great animation.

The Crinan Canal occupies a cutting nine miles long across the isthmus of Kintyre, linking the sea loch Fyne with the Sound of Jura to avoid the eighty-mile voyage around the Mull of Kintyre. It was constructed in 1801 by Telford, who had a hand in most of the civil engineering works of his time. A road accompanies the canal throughout its length.

Kintyre is a long pendant peninsula extending south from the mainland and ending within sight of Ireland. It is traversed by the A.83, joined soon after leaving Crinan. I have never been further along it than Tarbert, where the ferry leaves for Islay. With all due respect to Kintyre, which I am sure is a green and pleasant land, the prospect of spending a precious day on the fifty-mile journey to Campbeltown and fifty miles back without a mountain in sight has never appealed to me. Once committed to this long drive, the only escape from it occurs at one point where a car ferry crosses to Loch Ranza in Arran, and this I have pledged myself to do someday.

The A.816 becomes the A.83 beyond Crinan, the right fork heading for Tarbert and Campbeltown, the left bound for Inveraray, our next destination. The road at once passes along the main street of Lochgilphead where a long built-up seafront faces Loch Gilp, a minor arm of Loch Fyne.

Lochgilphead

Inveraray from the harbour

Leaving Lochgilphead behind, the road to Inveraray turns north-east alongside Loch Fyne. The immensity of this sea loch becomes apparent as the journey proceeds. It is one of the largest and longest of the inlets of the Atlantic, extending forty miles from the Sound of Bute into the heart of Argyll. It seems endless on the twenty-four miles to Inveraray; in places, the road turns inland and the loch is lost to sight for long distances but always it returns to find its waters still rolling on like Old Man River. In fact, one rather tires of the close company of Loch Fyne: it is not especially attractive, lacking the beauty of Loch Awe or the charm of Loch Maree, nor is there much of interest in the countryside bordering its waters. But feet are kept marching and wheels turning by the magnet of a fine group of mountains ahead. It is a relief to tedium when the neat streets of Inveraray are finally entered.

INVERARAY

Everybody halts at Inveraray. It is small, a town in miniature but a town nevertheless and a proud one, being a Royal Burgh with a long history and still the acknowledged capital of Argyll. In lovely grounds is the seat of the Dukes of Argyll, Inveraray Castle, open to the public. The setting of the town is delightful, the white buildings being backed by rich woodlands and colourful hills. There is a harbour on Loch Fyne alongside: it seems incredible that the waters are tidal so far from the sea. There are shops, accommodation and refreshments. Everybody halts at Inveraray.

Inveraray Castle   Opposite *Overlooking Loch Fyne at Inveraray*

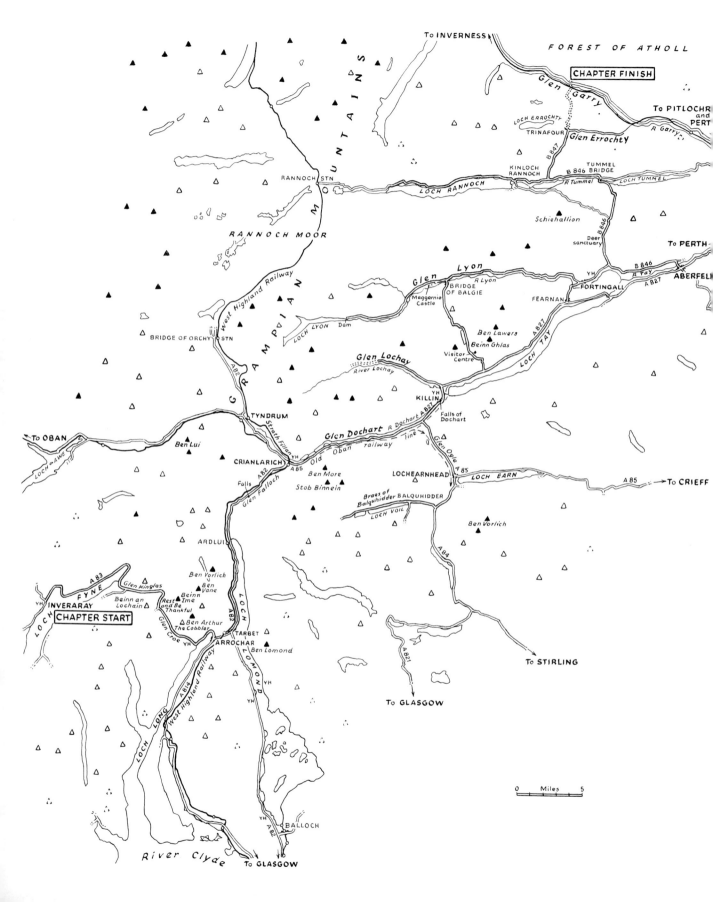

THE SOUTHERN HIGHLANDS

THE A.83 goes on beyond Inveraray, still unable to shake off Loch Fyne which persists alongside for a further six miles before finally giving up the ghost and expiring in a tidal swamp, whereupon the road crosses to the other side of the valley, as it has been wanting to do for some time, and returns south to a junction. Here, with a last farewell to Loch Fyne, the A.83 turns into Glen Kinglas towards an imposing knot of high mountains. High on the right are the menacing ramparts of Beinn an Lochain and, directly ahead, the shapely pyramid of Beinn Ime, seeming to bar further progress.

Beinn Ime

The Cobbler

To pass Beinn Ime, the road turns and slants up a long incline around its lower slopes, arriving at a pass still known as Rest and Be Thankful from the days when horses and carts struggled to make the ascent on dirt roads. It is a popular spot, fresh and open after the claustrophobic confines of Glen Kinglas, and a good springboard for climbing the Munros around. From the top of the pass, the A.83 descends the long and densely afforested valley of Glen Croe, a gloomy defile under its shroud of conifers; in places can be seen the old road up which men and horses toiled in the days of long ago.

Glen Croe debouches on the shore of Loch Long, another narrow inlet of the sea with a naval establishment concerned with the testing of torpedoes. The road turns alongside the water and, after a mile, a well-blazed track leaves it and climbs the hillside. Thousands of boots make their way up here every year alongside the Buttermilk Burn to an open prairie above from which springs a high ridge of naked rock, fantastically carved and an irresistible challenge to adventurers with red blood in their veins. This remarkable spine of rock is popularly known as The Cobbler, due to a fancied outline resemblance to a cobbler at his last; properly it is the summit of Ben Arthur. It is the most frequented of the mountaintops in the district and probably in all Scotland. The crest of the ridge can be gained by average walkers at one point of weakness but progress along it needs care; the buttresses are for expert cragsmen only.

Back on the A.83, the head of Loch Long is soon rounded and the large village of Arrochar is entered. Here we first become aware of the near proximity of Glasgow and the industrial towns of the Clyde and their influence on the way of life of this and other rural communities within easy reach of the many urban dwellers who seek a weekly escape to the countryside.

ARROCHAR

I remember Arrochar as a quiet village with few visitors but in recent decades it has become a rather garish holiday resort with cars and coaches cluttering the streets and its earlier charm and sweetness sacrificed. Crowds infest the steamer pier and the beach and the gift shops. There is a railway station at a higher level on the West Highland line, giving quick access for weekend throngs from the Clyde. Arrochar has changed for the worse.

But the village remains, as ever, a splendid centre for excursions to the hills which have long been a convenient playground for Glaswegian climbers. Apart from The Cobbler and the mountains at the head of Glen Croe, two other Munros, Ben Vane and Ben Vorlich, can be approached from a lane leaving the village to the north. A peak a day makes a good programme for mountain enthusiasts spending a week at Arrochar. Once, all visitors came wearing boots; now most come in slippers and sandals. But the mountains never change, bless them: they are the true treasures of Arrochar.

This is the most southerly point of the journey. There are too many people around for comfort, and a feeling persists that we are in the outskirts of Glasgow. Here it is time to face north and return to the Highlands. To do so, the A.83 must be followed uphill and over a low ridge, passing the railway station, and suddenly there comes into view a magnificent prospect of Loch Lomond immediately ahead and Ben Lomond rising in majesty from its far shore.

LOCH LOMOND

Loch Lomond is lovely, well deserving the countless ballads and poems and other eulogies it has inspired. Every one of its twenty-three miles is a joy to behold. On a bright day, the blue waters speckled with yachts, the many wooded islands and the colourful tapestries provided by the bonny banks and braes make a picture beyond compare, a canvas too large and too gracious to be affected by the irritation of traffic passing along its western margin in endless procession.

The south end of the loch, however, is not for those who prefer to appreciate beauty in silence. Only a few miles from the suburbs of Glasgow, and with industry and commerce encroaching, the southern fringes have been developed as car and coach parks, camping and caravanning sites and a marina for pleasure boats. Here are tawdry gift shops, ice cream, transistor radios, modern hotels, noise: the place is a happy playground for holidaymakers who like to congregate in crowds and have fun.

Here too is Balloch. I once spent a wretched night in Balloch. It was a long time ago but still sears my memory, and is worth telling you about.

Loch Lomond

Loch Lomond from Tarbet

I arrived in Balloch by bus in late afternoon and was given a room next to a w.c. which, in normal circumstances, I would regard as a convenient arrangement. But two coachloads of geriatric sightseers also arrived for an overnight stay, and although weaknesses of the bladder must be expected in old age, the whole party seemed to be leaking badly. Every few minutes, all night long, I heard the next door open and after a brief silence the chain being pulled with its sudden explosive noise of flushing water. My bed was against the dividing wall and my head only a matter of inches from the nerve-shattering eruption of the water system which, in the dead of night, was loud and startling. Fifty times at least this happened during the hours of darkness. There was no hope of sleep. To add insult to injury, I was greeted in the breakfast room by the happy faces and beaming smiles of those who had destroyed my sleep. I have never stayed overnight in Balloch since.

So, when the A.83 comes down to the lochside at Tarbet, our route joins the A.82 and turns north. This is the fifth Tarbet we have met on the journey, the name always signifying the presence of water and the situation usually being a narrow neck of land or isthmus, as in this instance, Loch Long and Loch Lomond being only a mile apart. Beyond Tarbet, the road and railway go hand in hand alongside the narrowing waters of the loch in beautiful scenery marred only by a hydro-electric complex fed by huge pipes coming down the hillside.

The road continues pleasantly to the head of Loch Lomond at Ardlui, which has a pier and a railway station in a setting of lovely trees. Then the road enters Glen Falloch, now having a charming river as a companion, while the gallant West Highland line pursues a resolute course through difficult terrain on the left, testifying to the skill of the Victorian engineers.

Ardlui

The Falls of Falloch

The road rises through the glen and on one sharp incline the verges have been scraped away by the parking cars and the tread of feet, indicating a popular halt and a sight worth seeing. A brief stroll through the trees to the river brings the Falls of Falloch into full view: a thrilling spectacle especially when in spate.

Further up the glen, in open country, remnants of the old Caledonian Forest are seen scattered on the bare hillsides as clumps of Scots pine, no longer standing proud and dignified as in ancient days but as lonely survivors, forlorn and sad. They have had their day.

The road crosses a low pass at the head of the glen and new landscapes come into view, everywhere mountainous, as it descends gently with the railway into Crianlarich.

Survivors of the Caledonian Forest

CRIANLARICH

When I first went to Crianlarich, I expected to find a town, my map telling me that there were two railway stations here and a junction of three major roads. Certainly it is a place of strategic importance but is not a town, merely a small village owing much to a favoured situation that might be claimed as a gateway to the Highlands. It opens the way to the western seaboard, the far north and the eastern Grampians. Since then, one of the railway stations has been closed: this served the Glasgow–Oban line, which made a circuitous journey by way of Callander and Glen Ogle and passed beneath the West Highland line at Crianlarich. In a major reconstruction, the Oban line now branches from the other in the village, the old track thus far having been torn up.

Crianlarich is a splendid base for mountaineering expeditions and for tours by car. The mountains are close at hand and can be reached without transport. The exciting Cruach Ardrain group was passed on the way into the village from Glen Falloch, the majestic Ben Lui is only a few miles to the west, and the great twins of Ben More and Stob Binnein rise from the valley immediately to the east. The village stands at a bend in a long trench, the western branch being Strath Fillan leading to Tyndrum and Rannoch Moor, the eastern having the name of Glen Dochart and pointing the way to Tayside. With Loch Lomond near to the south, sojourners at Crianlarich are really spoiled for choice.

I once spent a morning at Crianlarich kicking myself. I had stayed overnight at the hotel and had a wonderful day planned: I intended to catch the 8.30 train to Fort William, change there to the Mallaig train and sail by steamer to Kyle of Lochalsh, where I had a room booked in advance. After an early breakfast, I checked my watch with the hotel clock: both agreed the time as five minutes past eight as I paid my bill and went outside. Here, to my utter dismay, I saw the Fort William train crossing the viaduct after leaving the station, where I went to seek the truth. It was as I feared: I had made a stupid mistake. The scheduled time of departure was 8 o'clock, not 8.30 as I had wrongly supposed. There was not another train for Fort William until evening, the next being for Oban at midday from the other station. It was a sunny day but a dark cloud settled over me as I walked across to the Oban platform. What a stupid mistake and only myself to blame! I killed four hopeless and endless hours, and then, as the timetable promised, a train came and took me to Oban. From here, I sent a telegram to the hotel at Kyle, saying I had missed my train but would call later in the week. Then I took a train to Ballachulish on the now-defunct Lorn railway, and from there a bus to Fort William for the night.

Strath Fillan

Next day, I duly presented myself at the Kyle of Lochalsh Hotel and offered to pay for my cancelled booking, only to be told with a smile that there was no charge. I went away richer than I thought: on a previous stay at this hotel, the cost was three pounds a night, twice as much as I usually paid elsewhere. The lesson for me was always to check and double-check timetables when travelling in the Highlands by public transport, trains and buses being few and far between.

Opposite *The railway at Crianlarich*

Ben More

Our route from Crianlarich heads north-east along Glen Dochart on the A.85 and at once is confronted by the towering presence of Ben More, rising in a tremendous upward surge to its summit at 3843 feet, the slope thereto being at a gradient of 40 degrees without respite. I have a soft spot for Ben More, being another of the few Scottish mountains with a name I can pronounce with confidence, but affection does not extend to its ascent and descent. The climb directly from the road is an unremitting treadmill of 3300 feet with the toes pointing upwards every step of the way; the direct descent is the longest and most tedious in my experience, the slope being too steep for walking at a normal gait and progress only being possible by coming down sideways like a crab. The best route, up or down, lies along the glen to the west, aiming for the pronounced saddle between Ben More and Stob Binnein from which the top is easily gained.

Ben More is simple in design: a perfect cone without offshoots and ramifications and there are no problems of route finding or losing direction. On Ben More, you are either going steeply up or steeply down. The name means 'the Great Hill' and those who reach the summit cairn agree that it is well deserved.

Further along the road, after passing Ben More, maps draw attention to Rob Roy's Castle, perched on a nearby hillside, and curiosity impels a visit but it is found to be merely the pathetic ruin of a cottage with only one gable remaining intact and no evidence of any historical association. Rob Roy is to Scotland as Robin Hood is to England, the name appearing often and usually of doubtful authenticity.

Glen Dochart is a wide pleasant strath, mostly under cultivation and graced by a string of pretty lochs connected by the River Dochart. The old Oban railway follows the road closely before crossing it and maintaining a contour to Killin Junction Station. Here the main line turned south into Glen Ogle and a short branch went forward into Killin: all this railway activity has vanished and only the grass-grown tracks remain to tell of the happy and exciting days of steam trains. There is still a Killin junction but today it is a meeting of roads. Here the A.85 turns south into Glen Ogle, aiming for Callander and Stirling and the A.827 goes forward into Killin. The latter continues out itinerary, but a detour of a few miles along the A.85 introduces new landscapes of distinctive charm too attractive to be bypassed.

Ben Vorlich across Loch Earn

The A.85 first rises from the junction to a pass where a large car park invites travellers to enjoy a fine view of the Ben Lawers range and Loch Tay. Then follows a long descent of Glen Ogle, a wild defile, where the line of the abandoned railway can be seen bravely maintaining a straight course on the hillside through fields of boulders and across ravines to arrive with the road at Lochearnhead, a populated area – rather too populated by visitors to appeal to me but a convenient starting point for the ascent of Ben Vorlich, well seen across the busy marinas of Loch Earn.

Much more to my liking is the quiet and unspoiled valley of Balquhidder, branching off the road two miles further south and reached after passing more sad relics of the old railway that once gave me such excitement and pleasure.

A narrow road persists along this lovely glen for several miles to its head in a semicircle of peaks, these being the Crianlarich mountains seen from an unfamiliar direction. Loch Voil is a pleasing feature midway and here, too, are the heathery Braes of Balquhidder and the authentic grave of Rob Roy immortalised by Scott.

Loch Voil

KILLIN

Resuming the journey from the Killin road junction, the A.827, the abandoned railway track and the River Dochart proceed side by side to enter the delightful village of Killin, arriving there in surroundings of natural splendour. A picturesque bridge built in 1760 carries the road over the river and is a grandstand for admiring crowds looking over the parapet at an enthralling sight: the Falls of Dochart. Here the river, after a long and sedate journey, suddenly erupts in a furious rage, descending in a turbulent cataract of white foam along a wide and rocky channel in a remarkable display of thrashing waters. The flow of the rapids is interrupted by wooded islands, one of which was the burial place of the clan MacNab, and a bower of lovely trees enhances a scene of outstanding beauty, spectacular at all times and in periods of flood dramatic. It is an irresistible subject for the camera and the artist, but neither film nor canvas could ever reflect the overwhelming intensity of the Falls of Dochart.

The Falls of Dochart

The bridge at Killin

Recently, Killin has become a very popular place of resort for visitors who arrive in cars and coaches and in summer throng the main street, which has shops, ice cream vendors and tea rooms. Nearby is the head of Loch Tay, entered by the rivers Dochart and Lochay and offering a haven for pleasure craft.

Killin is an excellent centre for pedestrian expeditions since there is a choice of delightful walks, and for motorists who, within a radius of twenty miles, can visit two glens of supreme beauty. And, beckoning all, is Ben Lawers.

The head of Loch Tay

River Lochay

GLEN LOCHAY

The A.827 forms the main street of Killin and goes on around a corner to greet the River Lochay in parklike surroundings. Here a narrow road turns off into Glen Lochay and although it comes to a dead end and must be reversed, the walk or drive along it should not be missed. Beyond a hydro-electric complex, the glen narrows and the river scenery is charming, compelling many halts as the tree-lined waters leap and dance in ecstasy. Everything here, apart from the strip of tarmac, is as Nature intended it to be. The sylvan environment ends suddenly, the road becomes a cart track and ahead is revealed the bare and austere head of the valley in a ring of five Munros: a grim panorama in total contrast to the lower reaches. Glen Lochay, despite its nearness to Killin, is quiet and unfrequented. It should not be missed.

The head of Glen Lochay

BEN LAWERS

A few miles further along the A.827, a minor road branches to the left. It is heralded and proclaimed by large road signs that it is of great importance to the traveller. In fact, it is the innocent old road crossing over to Glen Lyon with no fuss at all, the reason for the signs being that the first two miles have been adopted as a route to a much-frequented Visitors' Centre. Normally I steer clear of Visitors' Centres and Leisure Centres, which too often are populated by noisy crowds. But this one has a particular merit: it introduces Ben Lawers to the public by word and picture with special mention of its Alpine flora, and describes the route of ascent. (Incidentally, the road – if continued to its end at the Bridge of Balgie in Glen Lyon – is a splendid alternative to continuing east along the A.827 for the next stage of the journey to Fortingall: it is narrow, steep and rather adventurous but very rewarding in scenic delights. Glen Lyon is described on pages 171 and 172 on the more usual approach from Fortingall.)

Ben Lawers is a mountain out of the ordinary. It rises to 3984 feet and remains officially at this height despite the occasional efforts of enthusiasts to add sixteen feet to the summit cairn. It is therefore one of the greats and a challenging objective of hill walkers. But it has a more important claim to fame as the habitat of a wealth of plant life including species not found elsewhere in the country and is of national renown and attracts botanists from far and wide. With a view to conserving the rare specimens, visitors whose aim is merely to get to the top of Ben Lawers are requested to keep strictly to the well-defined path, leaving the remote areas for the expert plant hunters. Even the much-trodden tourist path to the summit, however, has floral delights; in particular, the treadmill of the ascent is relieved by prolific clumps of the beautiful rose campion.

Ben Lawers has rewards all its own. There is the usual exhilaration of mountain climbing and the revelation of far-reaching panoramas, but something else. Flowers along the way.

Ben Lawers across Loch Tay

Beinn Ghlas

The route of ascent is well trodden and without difficulty other than steepness. The path leaves the Visitor Centre, crosses wet ground and then rises to a ridge of Beinn Ghlas, visiting its summit and descending slightly to a wide saddle beyond which is the summit pyramid of Ben Lawers, the path climbing steeply to its rocky top. The view is extensive in all directions, seemingly extending over half of Scotland. If a car was left at the Centre, the return must be made along the same path; if there is no such encumbrance, a descent may be made to the Lawers Hotel on the A.827.

The Visitor Centre for Ben Lawers

GLEN LYON

The A.827 continues along the base of Ben Lawers but elevated above Loch Tay, of which there are excellent views. This section, however, is bare and uninteresting until, after passing the Lawers Hotel, the road descends to the side of the loch in more attractive surroundings. At the village of Fearnan, the A.827 is left in favour of an unclassified road leading to Fortingall. Before reaching Fortingall, however, an insignificant fingerpost points the way to Glen Lyon along a minor road with the appearance of a private drive, and this should be followed for a half-day's detour of sustained delight. Glen Lyon is a lovely valley in a quiet and peaceful environment, blissfully free from caravans and commercialism and tourists in the mass; an Arcadia, a retreat for the connoisseur of natural beauty. Curiously, although giving access to one of the longest glens in the country, thirty miles from end to end, the entrance is so concealed and constricted that it is unsuspected and may be passed unnoticed. Glen Lyon gets little mention in guidebooks. Someone should sing its praises – but not too loudly.

The road through Glen Lyon is narrow and tortuous, and so luxuriantly screened by trees that views fore and aft are severely restricted. Only the mountains ranged on both sides are clearly seen above the canopies of foliage. Every turn of the tarmac reveals new scenes of rural charm. All is quiet and profoundly peaceful. Only the murmur of the river nearby and the twittering of birds disturbs the stillness, all else enjoys a siesta.

There are occasional crofts and cottages, a few large houses and estates, and much of the ground is fertile and pastoral.

After twelve miles, the road reaches the Bridge of Balgie.

River Lyon at the entrance to the glen   *The Bridge of Balgie*

The Bridge of Balgie carries the only other road in Glen Lyon across the River Lyon, this climbing over a bare moorland and descending past the Ben Lawers Visitors' Centre to the Killin–Aberfeldy road, the A.827. Beyond the bridge, the valley road rises past the picturesque castle of Meggernie and at the top of the gradient, now clear of trees, there are at last uninterrupted and distant views of the glen, both forward and in retrospect, and all is good to look upon. Around, and to the far horizon, are gaunt mountains.

On and on goes the road, writhing and twisting but always heading resolutely west as though engaged on some special mission, and so it proves when, after several more miles in increasingly wild terrain, it comes to an end at the dam of Loch Lyon. So far to the west has the glen penetrated that from this point a good walker could follow the lochside, cross a low ridge and pass under a viaduct of the West Highland Railway to reach food and drink at Bridge of Orchy in the space of three hours.

Wheels can go no further than the dam and motorists must turn their cars round and go back to Fortingall the way they came. Not many will begrudge the gallon of petrol it has cost them to make the long detour along Glen Lyon. Much more likely is that they will return, and often.

Glen Lyon

The Fortingall yew

Thatched cottages in Fortingall

FORTINGALL

Fortingall is a village of distinction, as pretty as a picture, a place of thatched cottages and flowery gardens and having in the churchyard a yew of immense girth, said to be the oldest tree in Scotland. There are Roman earthworks in the adjoining fields; also the birthplace, it is thought, of Pontius Pilate, a claim hard to believe but, if true, it must be said that he could not have entered the world in more beautiful surroundings. Here, in a fertile valley watered by the River Lyon and flanked by wooded heights, peace and tranquillity reign undisturbed. No wonder the villagers have smiling faces. Fortingall has an air of superiority and it is deserved.

Beyond Fortingall the road arrives at a T-junction, and here a short detour may be made for the replenishment of supplies by turning right along the B.486 for the few miles to Aberfeldy. This pleasant market town is entered by way of a particularly handsome bridge over the River Tay, attributed to General Wade and dated 1733. There are hotels and shops to meet all needs in Aberfeldy and a most delightful short walk through the riverside trees of the Birks that itself justifies the detour.

But from the Fortingall T-junction our route lies to the north, the road climbing steadily in a wooded countryside to more open ground where the great peak of Schiehallion may be glimpsed to the west. Still climbing, the road passes a deer sanctuary, which may be inspected, and then rises to the crest of a ridge where, from nearby eminences, the full length of Loch Rannoch may be seen. At this point, a path leads off for the ascent of Schiehallion by the gradual east ridge, much the easiest way up this fine mountain, which from other directions assumes the shape of a steep, perfectly formed pyramid.

Schiehallion across Loch Rannoch

Loch Rannoch

Ignoring a side road branching left to Kinloch Rannoch, our road goes forward on a long descent to the valley ahead, passing lovely birch woods and a huge hydro-electric building to cross the River Tummel by a modern bridge with a picturesque old bridge alongside. Here is another T-junction and, again, we prefer to turn left on the B.846 for a mile until arriving at a meeting of roads and a signpost pointing the way to Trinafour. A decision must be taken here. If time is not pressing, the B.846 may be followed into the village of Kinloch Rannoch and from there you can drive around the twelve-mile length of Loch Rannoch, there being motor roads on both sides and connecting at the head of the loch. The single road continues towards the wilderness of Rannoch Moor and comes to an end at the lonely Rannoch Station on the West Highland Railway.

Both sides of the loch are pleasantly wooded and the roads are quiet, enabling the scenery to be enjoyed without distraction, but Loch Rannoch has not the appeal for me that other lochs have, perhaps because of its use as a reservoir and its attendant works. Maybe I am too fussy, but I have always preferred Nature's designs to those of man.

The journey then continues along the B.847 road to Trinafour.

Birchwoods near Tummel Bridge   *Old and new at Tummel Bridge*

My preferred route, if the diversion around Loch Rannoch is not taken, climbs sharply, bordered by trees, to an open moorland, rich in heather and providing excellent retrospective views of Schiehallion and Loch Rannoch. It then joins the B.847 coming up directly from Kinloch Rannoch for the descent into Glen Errochty, arriving at the charming hamlet of Trinafour in a bower of trees, a quiet backwater with features of interest including a tiny church and a water-powered sawmill. Away from the usual tourist routes, Trinafour passes its days undisturbed.

The B.847 turns east to join the busy A.9 highway but a much more exciting and rewarding alternative is offered by a narrow moorland road, part of General Wade's Military Road, leaving Trinafour on the left: this climbs steadily northwards, becoming unfenced, and cars that survive two severe hairpin bends reach a broad expanse of heather with little roadside pools: heaven on a sunny day. And the views are far-reaching. Down on the left is the reservoir and manmade works of Loch Errochty, and then, as the highest point of the road is reached, a most wonderful panorama of the treeless Forest of Atholl is disclosed extending for many miles beyond the wide valley of another Glen Garry. Here are seen, due north, the mountains of Drumochter, Munros all, and to the east, the outliers of the Cairngorms, our rainbow's end but still very distant.

There are not many places in the Highlands where views are unobstructed by nearby mountains, but here they are, far away, etched against the sky beyond vast heather moors. This 'secret' road is one of my favourites, and it gradually descends to valley level, crossing the main Perth–Inverness railway near a signal box and the rocky and often dry bed of the River Garry, robbed of its water to serve the needs of man and, finally, amongst an oasis of trees, it filters onto the A.9.

Loch Tummel

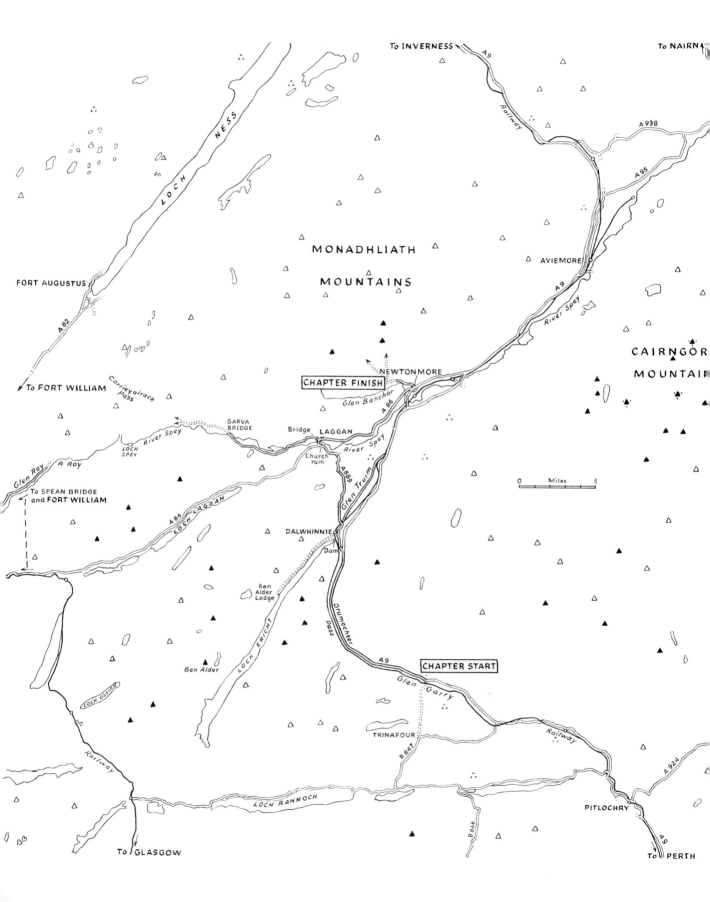

STRATH SPEY

THE A.9 merits a paragraph to itself. This is the main road artery to the north of Scotland and is very familiar to the many like myself whose regular tours of Scotland are the highlights of every year. In the past two decades, the road has been transformed by re-construction and re-alignment into a wide modern highway; every inch of the 114 miles from Perth to Inverness is brand new. Formerly, the A.9 passed through every one of the dozen towns and villages en route but now all are bypassed and connected by offshoots. Formerly there were hazards: snow on the Drumochter Pass, congestion in the village streets, heavy lorries impeding progress. Now there may still be snow at Drumochter – although its passage has been eased by a double carriageway – but all other difficulties have been smoothed away. Once there were 30-m.p.h. speed limits in all the built-up areas; today there are none, and amazingly there is not a single roadside building on the 114 miles from Perth to Inverness. The new road is a triumph of planning and engineering, splendidly graded, and a constant speed can be maintained throughout its length. The journey has become so free of impediments that there is more opportunity to appraise the wonderful scenery on all sides. After travelling on the old road for many years, I have found the changes that have taken place almost unbelievable and, although generally in favour of leaving things as they are, I must admit that the new A.9 is a major improvement and a great tribute to the men who planned and made it.

Alongside the A.9 almost all the way is the Perth–Inverness railway, an even greater achievement by the Victorian surveyors and engineers who faced and gallantly overcame the difficulties inherent in laying a line through mountainous terrain, the desolate Drumochter Pass being crossed at an altitude exceeding 1500 feet, the highest elevation of any railway in the British Isles. I have travelled on this line scores of times and never failed to be thrilled by the passing scenery; perpetually lost in admiration of the skill of the men who made it possible.

The Drumochter Pass on the A.9

Loch Ericht, from Dalwhinnie

DRUMOCHTER PASS

After the quiet crossing from Trinafour, the streams of fast-moving traffic on the A.9 will be met with some dismay, but the newly-structured road is able to cope easily with all demands and the long, gradual ascent to the Drumochter Pass is quickly and easily accomplished without even a change of gears. The pass is a scene of desolation, despite a few cottages and trees alongside the railway, and there is little temptation to linger. Stern and rather forbidding mountains form a backcloth to a dreary foreground but offer no invitations to climb to their summits. I have always stoutly maintained that all mountains are worth climbing, and so they are, but, to be honest, those overlooking Drumochter have always seemed brooding and hostile and I have never ventured amongst them – although with the advantage of a start at 1500 feet, only half their height need be climbed on foot. Maybe it is the depressing and unfriendly atmosphere of Drumochter that keeps wheels turning without a halt.

From the pass, there is a long descent at an even gradient into Glen Truim, leading into one of the best known of Scottish valleys, that of the River Spey, and after a few more miles of uninteresting travel, a branch road leaves for the first cluster of buildings: the village of Dalwhinnie, straggling the old A.9, a popular halt for coaches with its prominent distillery and hotels. But the attraction of Dalwhinnie for me, out of sight of the village street but only a good stone's throw distant, is Loch Ericht, reached by a private road alongside.

Loch Ericht is ended by a dam but when the water level is low, a stony beach is revealed where searchers after attractive pebbles and driftwood can spend an exciting hour in their pursuit. The loch is fifteen miles long, very narrow and deeply inurned amongst the mountains of a remote wilderness without habitations or communications.

And it points the way to Ben Alder.

BEN ALDER

I must admit that I never really got to grips with Ben Alder because of its extreme isolation and the difficulties of approach and ascent. It is the dominant height, rising to 3757 feet in a region remote from human influence, a confusing tangle of peaks a hundred square miles in extent without a road or a habitation: one of the greatest wildernesses in Scotland. The climbing of Ben Alder after a long and tiring walk to it was beyond my powers without an overnight bivouac, but my ambition was restricted merely to bringing it within easy range of my camera and even that simple objective was aborted and frustrated, so well shielded and hidden was it behind a ring of satellites. I tried approaching from Loch Ossian, from Loch Laggan and from Loch Rannoch, but to no avail, the ben being too shy to appear. I finally brought it into view by a long walk from Dalwhinnie along the five-mile private road to Ben Alder Lodge, thence continuing along a track to open country where its full stature was revealed.

Ben Alder must be regarded as out of bounds to all but supermen carrying tents or other protection against the weather. There is a natural shelter in Cluny's Cage, if it can be found: this was briefly tenanted by Bonnie Prince Charlie during his wanderings after defeat at Culloden. There is also an old bothy on the shore of Loch Ericht, this sometimes being used as a refuge.

If permission can be obtained to take a car along the private road to park at Ben Alder Lodge, a lovely oasis embowered in mature trees, it may be possible for a very strong walker to get to the summit of Ben Alder and return in the course of a long day; lesser mortals will be content to reach open country and see the mountain fully displayed but still distant and out of their reach.

From Dalwhinnie, instead of rejoining the A.9, take a rising road, the A.889, heading north. This provides an opportunity of seeing the upper valley of the River Spey and the mountains of Monadhliath – areas too often bypassed by tourists in haste to reach Aviemore or Inverness. The road crosses a wide ridge with distinctive foothills on either side and then gradually descends into a green basin occupied by the few cottages of Laggan and the River Spey, a beautiful picture of rural repose made all the more charming by the harsh mountain background.

The Upper Spey Valley

Garva Bridge

Acquaintance with the A.86 coming from Spean Bridge is resumed near a ruined church; at the foot of the descent, and half a mile forward the Spey is crossed at Laggan Bridge and Laggan is reached. An ancient and historic road diverges westwards from the A.86 here; this was constructed by General Wade for military operations and continues over the Corrieyairack Pass to Fort Augustus. For six miles out of Laggan, the road is surfaced for cars and it is a delightful drive to its end at Garva Bridge, built by Wade in 1732: it is a proud and picturesque structure spanning the Spey, here already a lusty infant. Cars may be parked at this attractive spot and legs exercised on an easy walk along the gravelly continuation of the military road towards the pass. Indeed, without too much effort, the Spey can be followed to its source in the little Loch Spey, by branching off the pass road two miles beyond the bridge on a rough track that keeps alongside the youthful stream to Loch Spey; this track goes on past a reconstituted bothy open to walkers and then enters Glen Roy, an exhilarating trek in open country.

Garva Bridge is a peaceful place for a siesta and the river is exciting but a return must be made to the A.86 at Laggan and then followed east into the main valley of the Spey at Newtonmore.

General Wade's road

Newtonmore is the first of a string of villages in the broad and beautiful valley of the Spey, one of the finest and best known of Scottish rivers, with catering and accommodation facilities for the many summer visitors attracted by the outdoor activities available in the neighbourhood. It has a railway station, and although no longer astride the A.9, easy access can be gained from the new main road. The bypass has given the villagers a quieter environment and possibly resulted in a loss of income for the shops and garages, but no doubt for many of the residents, tranquillity of life is worth more than pennies in the bank.

THE MONADHLIATH MOUNTAINS

Rising sharply to the north of Newtonmore is a group of mountains known as the Monadhliath. They do not attract attention from visitors hastening to the more popular and more exciting Cairngorms, and apart from the locals and holiday-makers staying at Newtonmore and, of course, once-in-a-lifetime visits by collectors of Munros, the area is largely unfrequented, being generally rounded in outline and lacking challenging cliffs and crags for the rockclimber. They are without distinction and character. Anyone wandering on their tops can be pretty sure of having them all to himself.

The Monadhliath Mountains

An easy approach to the group is offered by a narrow no-through-road leaving the village to the north and turning into Glen Banchor which is wooded and pastoral, and leads directly to the wild heart of the group; it is pierced by side glens bringing streams down from the heights. The mountains rise to the west and north and are relatively close together, making easy prey for the Munro-bagger. Glen Banchor is hidden from the main valley of the Spey by an intervening ridge and is unsuspected, adding to its charm.

Archaeologists in search of relics of long ago have a special interest in the Monadhliath. On their southern slopes are the ruins of ancient homesteads and the site of a village settlement, testifying to the occupation of the area in times long forgotten.

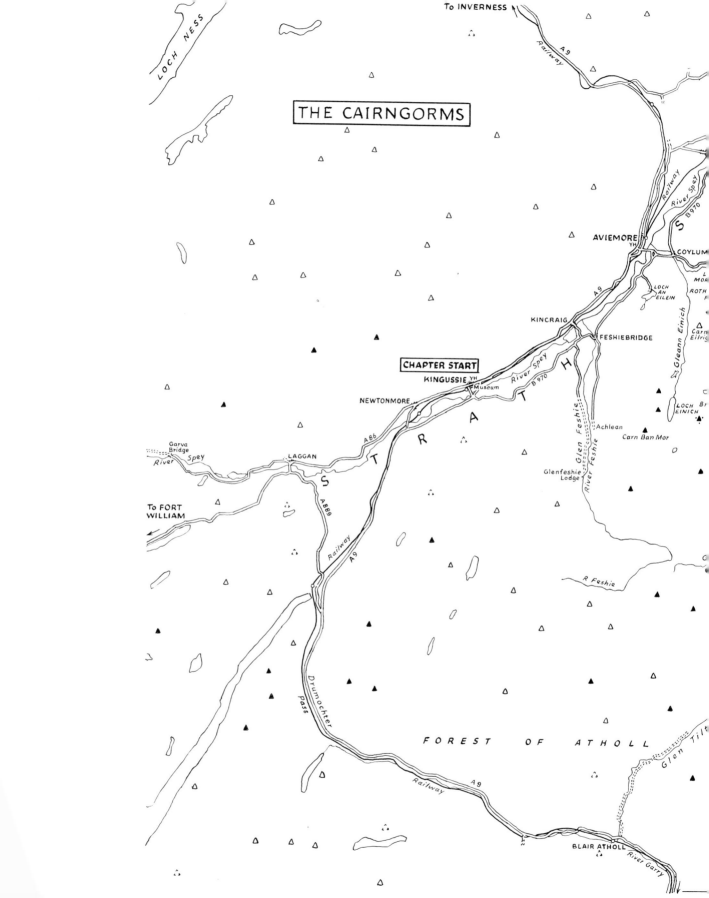

THE CAIRNGORMS

THE HIGHEST land mass in Scotland and the greatest in extent is a wilderness area of some two thousand square miles at elevations that are subject to Arctic conditions. It is situated between Strath Spey in the north and Glen Shee in the south, the western boundary being defined by the railway over Drumochter Pass and the eastern by Deeside. Regions within this area have distinctive names but the whole is loosely referred to as the Cairngorms.

The mass takes the form of a plateau with its main tops exceeding 4000 feet in altitude, dissected by deep glens that give access to the interior on rough tracks. There is only one public through road, this skirting the eastern fringe. All else is an upland desert. The Cairngorms have always been regarded as the exclusive preserve of experienced mountaineers and strong walkers, and the toll of casualties is a warning to others not to venture into the remoter fastnesses. Within the perimeter, there are no fewer than fifty-four Munros, many of them difficult to attain. This is not country for novices.

Since the war, the Cairngorms have acquired a reputation as the best of all British resorts for skiers and their pastime has been rapidly developed by the provision of chair-lifts and ski-tows on the slopes most conveniently accessible, notably in the districts of Aviemore and Glen Shee. Indeed, the Cairngorms are now better known for winter sports than for summer expeditions. But the mountains remain, as ever, notoriously dangerous for ill-equipped parties. The difficulties of mountain travel should never be under-estimated, in the Cairngorms especially. Some parts are best left to the herds of red deer who roam the hillsides: here is their home and man is an intruder.

The Cairngorms

Newtonmore is on the threshold of the Cairngorms and by continuing along the old A.9, the small town of Kingussie is reached and passed through. This is a sophisticated and popular resort with excellent facilities for visitors, including a Highland Folk Museum and charming amenities. It is the 'capital' of Strath Spey, as the valley of the Spey is named, with a well-kept railway station and access roads to the new A.9.

Beyond Kingussie is the smaller residential village of Kincraig, and it is here that the main stream of traffic is left behind as we follow a minor road to Feshiebridge to commence an exploration of the mighty Cairngorms.

Feshiebridge is a delightful spot, the River Feshie here hurrying beneath a fine old road bridge, shaded by lovely pines, to meet the Spey.

With my wife, I once rented a cottage here for a week. It had been advertised in a newspaper by the absentee landlord. The cottage was detached and isolated, charmingly named Heather Brae, and occupied a beautiful position with a convenient telephone box on the verge outside. It was paradise – until entered, when we found it to be dirty, ill-furnished and lacking necessary items. Upstairs were three broken bedsteads, nothing else; we carried the one least wrecked downstairs and never again went back upstairs, the rooms there being untenable. It was a lovely week but there was no pleasure in arriving 'home' after a long day's walking and we spent the evenings café-crawling. Moral: always look before you say yes.

Woods at Feshiebridge

GLEN FESHIE

Coming from the west, the first great opening in the mountain barrier is Glen Feshie, a beautiful valley not improved by conifer plantations in its lower reaches. From the B.970 one mile west of the bridge, a narrow road turns off and leads south into the glen, its objective obscured by trees at first, but once clear of these the valley is revealed as wide and spacious and continuing for many miles ahead. With the River Feshie alongside, the narrow strip of tarmac goes on and on, quiet and free from traffic, to end at Glenfeshie Lodge. Thus far, the scenery has been pleasant and pastoral, but now the glen narrows between rough slopes as the river emerges from a ravine and the glen turns a corner to its headwaters in the east.

Unlike most glens, which are terminated by mountains, Glen Feshie breaches the high ground and continues to rise gently to a watershed, declining beyond to the gathering grounds of the River Dee. There is thus a through route for walkers from Feshiebridge to Braemar avoiding any arduous climbing and giving an exhilarating crossing from one major river system to another. The watershed itself is a topographical curiosity. The River Feshie comes down to it from high ground to the south, heading east but, at the watershed, turns sharply west to enter Glen Feshie. A short distance across the flat watershed, the Geldie Burn starts its descent to Deeside. Both on the ground and on the map, it appears that the infant River Feshie once joined forces with the Geldie Burn to flow eastwards. A footbridge across the river at Glenfeshie Lodge gives access to the rough track, a right of way, leading in due course to Braemar.

Feshie Bridge

Glen Feshie

Glen Feshie is bordered by a range of mountains on its east flank and by low hills on the west. Although the mountains have the status of Munros, they lack distinction, being rounded in outline and linked by smooth ridges at a high level. When seen from the valley, therefore, they have the appearance of rolling moorlands of dreary aspect with no promise of interest or excitement and no inviting challenge.

The highest summit on the range is Carn Ban Mor, 3443 feet, and if it is desired to climb a mountain while in Glen Feshie, this is the one. The ascent, taking advantage of a good stalkers' path, is simple, with no steep gradients, but the tedium of the uphill trudge vanishes on reaching the ridge just below the summit when a tumult of peaks is suddenly revealed ahead, the view including many of the Cairn-gorm giants.

The ascent is made from the farming croft of Achlean on the east side of the River Feshie, reached by an access road from Feshiebridge, and thence by a distant path.

Loch an Eilein

The B.970 continues north-east from Feshiebridge in sylvan surroundings bound for Aviemore, but when a side road signposted Loch an Eilein branches to the right, it should certainly be followed to its end at a car park near this most beautiful and romantic of small lochs, a favourite objective of visitors staying in the district. In fact, this lovely spot is a victim of overkill, testified by erosion, tree damage, litter and noise. But the scenery transcends the irritations of too many sightseers and in early morning or late evening when left in undisturbed peace, the outlook across the water to the fourteenth-century castle on an island, now a gaunt ruin, and the heathery slopes beyond, has the added charm of solitude. The area is in the care of the Nature Conservancy who have fashioned a nature trail around the shores of the loch. More serious walkers with time to spare can make a foray into Gleann Einich from the lochside.

GLEANN EINICH

A clear path departs from the eastern shore of Loch an Eilein and enters the fringe of the magnificent Forest of Rothiemurchus amongst noble pines and rampant heather in the direction of Carn Eilrig.

Gleann Einich is a parallel valley to Glen Feshie but totally different, the entrance being constricted, the floor of the valley narrower and hemmed in by steep slopes and the scenery wilder. Nevertheless, a fair track continues along it for six miles to its dramatic end at Loch Einich deeply cradled between towering cliffs.

The path into Gleann Einich

Loch Einich

The path from Loch an Eilein becomes enchanting as it enters the forest and winds through heather with scattered pines masking the course of the River Einich but, after passing Carn Eilrig, it reaches a wild and treeless zone with rough slopes crowding in. The good track, however, encourages further progress and, indeed, the walking remains easy, transferring to the east bank of the river when a wooden bridge provides the unexpected luxury of a dry crossing. The massive shapeless bulk of Braeriach, at 4248 feet one of the Cairngorm giants, dominates the scene ahead, but as Loch Einich comes into sight it is the shattered cliffs plunging into its waters from the west that arrest the attention most, adding high drama to a scene of grandeur with desolation as its theme.

Walkers with cars parked at Loch an Eilein must retrace their steps exactly to claim their own and can then go into Aviemore by road; others may vary the later stages by an alternative path that reaches Aviemore by way of Coylumbridge.

AVIEMORE

I remember Aviemore when it was merely a small village consisting of rows of cottages and two hotels lining a main road, then the A.9. There was a large railway station which, in those days, served as a junction. Visitors arriving by train invariably wore heavy boots and tweeds and carried haversacks: they came for the sport of mountain climbing. Aviemore was a quiet place, in tune with the natural scenery around.

Since then, it has been changed out of all recognition and not for the better. It has fallen victim to commercial interests and has become a leisure centre de luxe, a massive development of skyscraper hotels and shops and restaurants with an artificial ski slope and all the fun of the fair. It has become a popular holiday resort catering for all types of visitor. Those wearing boots are in a minority, sandals and fancy footgear are more likely to be seen and T-shirts and shorts have replaced the tweed jackets and knickerbockers of the pioneers; handbags are the order of the day, not rucksacks. Old-timers feel aliens in a jungle of concrete. The place has become brash, garish, noisy. A new and growing influx of visitors are the skiers who, aided by chair-lifts and ski-tows, practise their sport on the mountain slopes; they form the bulk of the transient winter population and have earned for the Cairngorms a reputation as the best skiing centre in Britain. Aviemore is now busy both in summer and winter.

Nothing that has taken place here, however, can mar the grandeur of the environment: the majesty of the mountains, the superb scenery of Rothiemurchus Forest and Loch Morlich. Commercialism has spread into the countryside, and roads have been made and extended to take motorists to new car parks, but these are insignificant pinpricks in the vast scale of the Cairngorms landscape. Of course, the mountains remain open to the adventurous climber and complete freedom can be enjoyed there, as ever, and wanderings in the lonely recesses of Rothiemurchus Forest are no less delightful.

The most popular of the mountains, because of convenient access, is Cairn Gorm, which has given its name to the group of high peaks in the area. Its northern face is scarred by a huge car park, a double chair-lift and ski-tows, and the path to the summit is badly eroded by the tread of many boots. On the top, all is as it always was, except for the crowds: the vast panorama comprises a wilderness of high undulating ground, the greatest upland desert in Scotland. This is wonderful and exhilarating territory for the experienced walker, a dangerous playground for the inexperienced. The Cairngorms can be brutal if not treated with respect.

Aviemore is a sad example of the encroachment of man into the realms of natural beauty. I could never stay there again in its modern atmosphere of razzmatazz and blaring radios and crowded streets. It is best left to those who like such things. Those who remember the Aviemore of fifty years ago will bypass the babel of noise and head straight for the silent and unchanging Cairngorms, which rank amongst the finest mountains in the country and give real, not artificial, pleasure.

THE FOREST OF ROTHIEMURCHUS

Now partly a Nature Reserve, the great Forest of Rothiemurchus is the largest and finest surviving remnant of the original Caledonian Forest that once covered much of the Highlands and cloaks the valley south of the Spey from Loch an Eilein to Loch Morlich in a wealth of noble old pines carpeted

The Forest of Rothiemurchus

by heather and juniper, putting to shame some conifer plantations recently interspersed. Nature has been bountiful here and the combination of lovely trees, woodland glades and cascading streams backed by colourful and craggy hillsides makes a scene of surpassing beauty. Walking in the forest on its maze of paths is a joy.

THE LAIRIG GHRU

The best known of all Scottish foot-passes is the Lairig Ghru, linking Strath Spey and Deeside, a distance of twenty-four miles from Aviemore to Braemar and involving 2200 feet of ascent. The walking can be shortened by using transport on motor roads at both ends but it must always be an arduous marathon, not to be undertaken lightly. The Lairig Ghru bisects the Cairngorms, passing between the highest and most imposing mountains in the group and, in graphic scenery, follows the River Dee from its lonely and inhospitable birthplace in a wilderness of shattered rocks and scree fallen from the heights around.

The Lairig Ghru is for heroes and heroines.

CAIRN GORM

Cairn Gorm is a mountain that draws people like a magnet, largely because of the facilities of access it provides, partly because of the ease of ascent, partly because of the superb panorama from the summit and partly because everybody else goes there.

The Cairngorms from Loch Morlich

A road leaves Coylumbridge and enters the beautiful wooded Glen More, passing Loch Morlich, a popular resort of amateur mariners, and then climbs steadily up the side of the mountain to a large car park. A chair-lift starts nearby and, in two stages, conveys visitors to within a ten-minute walk of the summit. I don't like to see chair-lifts on mountains, although I am becoming more tolerant as legs begin to falter in old age. In this instance, however, I would recommend its use in preference to trudging up the stony path in the midst of the usual ragged procession with their transistor radios.

The view from the top makes it all worth while.

The view south-west from Cairn Gorm

The prospect from the summit of Cairn Gorm, at 4084 feet, is far reaching in all directions, almost overwhelming in its immensity, and displays a total contrast between the soft loveliness of Glen More and Strath Spey northwards, and the harsh wilderness suddenly revealed in the southern arc of the panorama: it is this latter aspect that most rivets the attention. All the major peaks of the Cairngorms are seen in crowded assembly, separated by deep glens, extending from Ben Avon in the east to Braeriach in the west: a vast array in a savage landscape. The highest of the group, Ben Macdui, fills the horizon due south.

Invariably the summit is inhabited by chattering and often noisy visitors but their company can be avoided by walking on a few hundred yards until they are lost to sight and sound, and the mighty grandeur of the scene can be surveyed in silence, as it should be for full appreciation.

The view south-east from Cairn Gorm

Walkers who have reached the top of Cairn Gorm the easy way, by chair-lift, thus conserving their energy, may feel inclined to undertake a visit to a neighbouring summit. Ben Macdui is an obvious objective, not too far away and easy of access with a minimum of ups and downs. This is a practicable proposition in fair conditions, but it must be borne in mind that distances in the Cairngorms are always greater than they look and that the onset of bad weather can cause confusion and difficulties in the absence of landmarks and that exposure at high altitudes is a danger to the unfit and unprepared. There have been many cases of parties getting into trouble on these inhospitable heights. The Cairngorms should never be under-estimated.

One walk, however, can be unreservedly recommended to average walkers: this goes south-west along the edge of the mountain overlooking Glen More to the subsidiary summit of Cairn Lochan, two miles distant, where a wild downfall of cliffs provides the most dramatic feature of Cairn Gorm.

THE PASS OF RYVOAN

An attractive short walk abounding in interest leaves the road to the Cairn Gorm car park beyond Loch Morlich and goes forward up the valley to the old Glenmore Lodge, now a youth hostel, and enters an area devoted to the training of young people in outdoor activities sponsored by the Scottish Sports Council who have built a new Glenmore Lodge for the purpose and provided a camp site. For the older visitor, there is an exhibition under the auspices of the Forestry Commission and a unique opportunity to see a herd of reindeer, a species imported from Lapland some thirty years ago and now thriving as exiles in a new land.

Reindeer in Glen More

An Lochan Uaine

The scenic delights of the Ryvoan walk come after the human and animal occupants of Glen More are left behind and a gravel road is followed onwards amongst lovely trees to come alongside the beautiful An Lochan Uaine, sometimes referred to as the Green Lake because of the unusual brilliance and translucent colour of its waters, a legendary home of fairies. In this enchanted spot, it is easy to believe in fairies.

Beyond An Lochan Uaine, the road leads up through the miniature Pass of Ryvoan, a narrow and rocky defile softened by foliage, and suddenly emerges at the top of the rise into bare moorland with a new landscape revealed ahead across the wide basin of the River Nethy to the rising slopes and stark summit of Bynack More.

For those with cars parked in Glen More, the walk ends at a bothy open for public use as a shelter or overnight refuge. For others, the track may be followed further to Nethy Bridge.

The Ryvoan bothy (left) *with Bynack More behind*

River Nethy

LAIRIG AN LAOIGH

The Pass of Ryvoan also makes an excellent prelude to a marathon trek from Glen More through the mountains to Deeside and Braemar, a route named Lairig an Laoigh and, like its counterpart, the Lairig Ghru, is a full day's expedition for strong and experienced walkers only.

Near the Ryvoan bothy, a track branches to the right and, after crossing the River Nethy, joins a path coming from Abernethy, then continuing below Bynack More to thread a lonely passage between towering heights in the heart of the eastern Cairngorms to emerge finally at Derry Lodge, Braemar being ten miles further by road.

The Lairig an Laoigh is a wild crossing amongst unfrequented mountains in scenery akin to that of the Lairig Ghru although less spectacular, but its remoteness and absence of shelter have never won it the same popular favour. In bad weather, it is out of the question.

It is time to move on. I have left myself only about thirty pages to cross over to glorious Deeside and describe the joys to be found there, and the superb scenery and excitement of the southern Cairngorms around Braemar, where our itinerary ends.

Walkers can cross the Cairngorms by either of the two Lairigs, but for motorists there is no direct way and a roundabout route must be followed, this happily having much of interest.

If returning from Cairn Gorm or Ryvoan, there is no need to go back into Aviemore to continue the tour; the B.970, a quiet road, leaves Glen More at Coylumbridge and soon comes alongside the Spey, travelling with it to the village of Boat of Garten, so named in the days when a ferry crossed the river at this point; this was later replaced by a bridge. Boat of Garten has one unique attraction that has won fame in newspaper headlines. It is where the ospreys live.

The River Spey at Boat of Garten

Loch Garten

ABERNETHY FOREST

Boat of Garten is on the fringe of the vast Abernethy Forest, rivalling Rothiemurchus Forest in extent and similarly having some fine stands of native pine. In its depths, near the shore of Loch Garten, is the first nesting site adopted by the ospreys a few decades ago upon their return to Scotland after a long exile. Their nests are jealously guarded by wardens, who permit access to viewing stations a hundred yards distant but otherwise keep the public at bay. A forest road, open for motor cars, leads to the site from the village.

I find it more satisfying to visit the home of the ospreys than to watch for the monster in Loch Ness. At least here there is something to see even if the birds are away on their daily round of hunting for fish.

A rather special place.

The ospreys' nest in Abernethy Forest

The ruins of Castle Roy

From Boat of Garten, the B.970 goes on to the next village down the valley, Nethy Bridge, situated on the River Nethy near its confluence with the Spey. It is a pleasant resort with a growing reputation as a centre for sporting activities. In the vicinity are delightful riverside and woodland walks, one leading to the historic ruin of Castle Roy.

Abernethy Forest extends far to the south and east and initially has a maze of paths suitable for half-day and evening strolls. One path, however, is more purposeful, heading through the forest and following the River Nethy to its distant source among the eastern Cairngorms: this is an alternative start to the thirty-mile march to Braemar by way of the Lairig an Laoigh, a gruelling trek for which an early morning start is essential.

The Lairig an Laoigh path in Abernethy Forest

The main street of Grantown-on-Spey

GRANTOWN-ON-SPEY

Still following the course of the River Spey, the B.970 leads into the small planned town of Grantown-on-Spey, which can be bypassed from Nethy Bridge but deserves a visit and a look around. There is much to admire in its well laid out streets and river environs, and the general air of community care. This is not a town with an ancient foundation, dating only from 1776, and its buildings are almost entirely of clean granite that has survived the ravages of weather for two centuries remarkably well, albeit aided by the house-proud concern of the inhabitants for civic tidiness. Grantown-on-Spey makes a good impression on visitors.

Ever since Garva Bridge near Laggan, the River Spey has been a delightful travelling companion, often coming alongside to display its charms, on occasion roaming out of sight but always returning to contribute added pleasure to the journey along its beautiful valley.

But at Grantown-on-Spey, farewells must be said. Here, forty miles distant from the Drumochter Pass, is the first opportunity to cross the immense bulk of the Cairngorms by road. Here the A.939 starts on a long and tortuous switchback journey over a bare plateau on the eastern fringe of the high Cairngorms, generally maintaining a high altitude but in places dropping sharply to cross valleys formed by the rivers born in this upland wilderness.

At the end of it is Deeside.

River Spey

Avon Bridge near Tomintoul

Soon after leaving Grantown-on-Spey, the A.939 enters a different landscape in significant contrast to the lovely woodlands and emerald pastures of Strath Spey, a landscape that becomes harsher and bleaker as mile succeeds mile on a rising course to a vast sweep of rolling moorlands ahead; south-west is the lofty skyline of the Cairngorm range. Trending east to give the mountains a wide berth, the road crosses the River Avon on its way to the fastnesses of Ben Macdui where it joins the River Spey in a friendlier environment and empties its waters in the Moray Firth.

Next along the road comes an unexpected surprise for motorists who do not trouble to study their maps. This is the large village of Tomintoul, 1160 feet above sea level and the highest village in the Highlands, and situated in such seemingly inhospitable surroundings that one wonders how it came to be there at all. But first impressions deceive. Tomintoul, favoured by anglers, is a sophisticated resort with hotels, shops and a youth hostel, and although out on a limb in the midst of a great wilderness is sturdily independent, as indeed it has to be in winter when the road is often blocked by snow.

Tomintoul

Beyond Tomintoul, the road starts a long incline through increasingly bare and desolate terrain to reach its highest point at 2090 feet, this section being known as the Lecht Road, originally constructed for military purposes. Then follows a long and steep descent to Cock Bridge and the River Don, another of the great waterways draining east from the Cairngorms. The bridge gets its name from a nearby hillock, the Cock. Nearby, the attractive Corgarff Castle is well worth a visit.

At Cock Bridge, the road turns east to keep company with the Don, but after two more miles, at a junction, forsakes it and heads south for Deeside, leaving the B.973 to continue alongside the river. Eight miles further, still in hilly country, the main road reaches Gairnshiel Bridge. The river flowing below it has special interest as it is a tributary of the River Dee, the first suggestion after travelling forty miles from Grantown-on-Spey that arrival on Deeside will not be delayed much longer. Over the bridge, the road forks and a choice must be made between the old military road, the B.976, going straight ahead and descending to Crathie and Balmoral, and the A.939 which follows the river down Glen Gairn and reaches the valley of the Dee at Ballater. Our preference is for the latter, deferring a visit to Balmoral until Ballater has been visited. Either route is a transition from wild uplands to sylvan beauty. After the rigours of the Lecht Road, Deeside is an enchanted fairyland.

Corgarff Castle

The railway station, Ballater

BALLATER

Ballater is a small, very attractive town, the 'capital' of Upper Deeside, delightfully situated in a curve of the River Dee amongst wooded hills and dominated by the mighty Lochnagar. The main valley road, the A.93, passes through the town which can be bypassed by through traffic, but all visitors should enter and perambulate through the streets and by the riverside, and they will immediately be aware of many evidences of civic pride. Everything is neat, clean and tidy. I remember the former railway station, terminus of an abandoned line from Aberdeen, as a floral garden, all scrupulously neat, its platforms clean as new pins: it was a pleasure to wait for a train here. It is a town graced by Royal favours and does its best to deserve them. Many of the shops bear insignia as suppliers to the Royal Family.

Ballater is very conscious of the presence of Balmoral Castle a few miles along the road, and preens itself in the grand manner on the occasions of Royal visits. There is no atmosphere of serfdom, only a deep respect and a dignified satisfaction that kings and queens should choose to make this beautiful valley their summer home.

Ballater folk love Ballater.

River Dee at Ballater

Ballater

Above *Lochnagar*

Below *The Falls of Muick*

GLEN MUICK

The environs of Ballater abound in lovely walks and excursions by car, but one expedition in particular should not be missed. A bridge crosses the River Dee to the B.976 and, from this, an unclassified road branches off into Glen Muick. An elaborate roadside memorial with Royal associations is passed and the road then follows a delightful drive up the valley with the River Muick which descends alongside in a tumble of cascades and waterfalls on its hurried journey from the mountains; dense forests lie on both flanks.

Loch Muick

After nine miles, the road reaches Spittal of Glenmuick and ends at a large car park. In more open country now, there is a splendid prospect ahead, the centrepiece being Loch Muick, introduced to television audiences by Prince Charles a few years ago; at the far end of the loch in a screen of trees is the Royal residence of Glas-allt Shiel. Beyond, closing the horizon, is the high skyline of Broad Cairn. Rising to the south of the loch is the moorland of the Capel Mounth, but it is to the west that most eyes turn, hoping for a close-range view of Lochnagar; actually the range is too close, foreshortening it and an intervening hillside masking the true glory of this noble mountain, one of the best known of Scottish peaks, proud to have enjoyed Royal patronage.

LOCHNAGAR

The ascent of Lochnagar is usually made from the car park at Spittal of Glenmuick by a path passing through a small plantation and then climbing without respite up a steep hillside. The tedium of the ascent is suddenly dispelled upon reaching the edge of a vast corrie ringed by precipitous cliffs, with the little Loch Nagar cradle below a downfall of scree. The scene is tremendously impressive, awesome and rather frightening. This is by far the finest aspect of the mountain and the faint-hearted need go no further. As they turn tail and flee in horror, however, they need reminding that Queen Victoria, handicapped by voluminous skirts, climbed to the top of the mountain in 1848, although admittedly by a less forbidding approach. Experienced walkers, however, will have no difficulty in making their way upwards and along the rim of the cliffs to the highest of the two summits at 3786 feet, and from there will enjoy a beautiful and extensive view of Deeside and the distant Cairngorms.

CAPEL MOUNTH

Another splendid walk available from the car park at Spittal of Glenmuick leads over the moorland south-east of Loch Muick and descends to Glen Doll and Glen Clova. It is known as the Capel Mounth and is a good example of the ancient rights of way used as drove roads for sheep and as packhorse routes. Their use has been continued by walkers, to whom they are a great help in crossing difficult terrain.

The Capel Mounth path slants upwards from the near end of the loch and affords excellent views as height is gained, both of the mountains around the head of the loch and of Lochnagar, here seen in better perspective.

I was once coming over the Capel Mounth from Glen Doll with my wife on a bright day that held no threat of bad weather, when, all of a sudden and literally out of the blue, we were enveloped in a grey mist and assailed by a furious downpour that fell upon us with the ferocity of a tornado. I have never suffered such an experience elsewhere. I was ill-clad for withstanding the onslaught: the rain attacked us with an intensity so fierce that within two minutes I was a soaking rag, with pockets full of water, ruining cigarettes and matches, and rivulets trickling down my bosom. It was impossible to proceed, or even to talk; all we could do was to crouch on the path and present as little surface as possible to the elements. I really thought the end had come for us – and was rather annoyed about this because I had wanted to die within sight of the Lakeland fells, not here on the Capel Mounth.

Then, within two more minutes, the rain stopped as quickly as it had begun, the mist drifted away, the sun shone and Lochnagar smiled at us under a cloudless blue sky.

My wife had fared rather better, having only half the surface exterior of myself, but we were both dripping water as we hurried down to the car park where picnickers, who had had unbroken sunshine, looked at us as though we were bedraggled monsters just emerged from the loch. We lay in the hot sun under twin clouds of steam until we dried out. I am convinced that we were victims of a local tornado. Lessons: always carry waterproof clothing on hillwalking expeditions, and keep cigarettes and matches in a watertight tin.

BALMORAL CASTLE

The next compulsive stop is at Balmoral, eight miles up the valley from Ballater, and there is a choice of roads to it: the main A.93 road goes along the north bank of the River Dee and the B.976 along the south bank, the latter being quieter, more free of traffic and to be preferred. The two roads converge just before Balmoral Castle.

The castle is a Royal residence of Her Majesty the Queen. It stands on the site of a medieval castle and was first visited by Queen Victoria in 1848. She fell in love with its glorious situation on a curve of the Dee, as do all who go there, and in 1852 the estate was purchased by the Prince Consort who rebuilt the castle in Scottish style to its present noble proportions. Adjoining properties, notably the natural woodland of Ballochbuie Forest, were added to the estate later. This part of the valley became known as Royal Deeside, and there is no fairer place on earth. Even the surroundings have majesty, the stately parklands being overlooked by heathery hills bearing large cairns on their summits to indicate favourite viewpoints of members of the Royal Family in earlier years. The whole scene has a mystical aura of romance. Balmoral Castle is a shrine to which the Royalist faithful pay reverent homage and it is a Mecca for visitors from other countries.

The grounds of the castle are generally open to the public when the Royal Family is not in residence. The many coaches and cars occupying the parking places and lining the adjacent roads bear testimony to the unique attraction of Balmoral Castle and, I think, of the affection felt for its Royal occupants. One comes away feeling highly privileged.

On the A.93 nearby is Crathie Church, a humble place of worship attended by members of the Royal Family when staying at Balmoral, and on such occasions a full house is assured.

Everybody is a Royalist when visiting Royal Deeside.

River Dee at Balmoral   *Crathie Church*

Balmoral Castle

Below *Woods near Balmoral*

From Balmoral, the A.93 heads south-west for many more sylvan miles alongside the River Dee and Ballochbuie Forest, a journey of sustained delight that irresistibly halts the wheels of the car for a leisurely appraisal of the lovely river and the scenic joys around. This kaleidoscope of colour and beauty comes to a grand culmination at the Old Bridge of Dee at Invercauld, a picturesque arched structure dating from 1753, recently repaired and rightly closed to traffic. With the forest rising behind and overtopped by the outliers of Lochnagar, the bridge poses perfectly for the artist with canvas or camera.

Just beyond the Old Bridge of Dee, the river is crossed at Invercauld Bridge from which there is a fine view of Lochnagar soaring majestically above the valley forests. Then the road runs along the base of a rugged height on the left, this featuring a crag known as the Lion's Face because of a similarity of profile. Further, on the right in lovely grounds, is Braemar Castle, sturdy, handsome and typically Scottish. It dates from 1628 and was rebuilt in 1748: it is open to the public.

The Old Bridge of Dee

Braemar Castle

BRAEMAR

The first buildings of Braemar are now in sight and the village is entered quietly, without any fanfare of trumpets, to complete our tour of the places in Scotland I have loved so much over many years. Braemar is journey's end, the foot of the rainbow, and the crock of gold is a wealth of scenic beauty in landscapes of unsurpassed grandeur. Braemar is an epitome of the best of Scotland. Here is a glorious river, hurrying in youthful exuberance from a lonely infancy; here are heather-clad hills and a towering backcloth of gaunt mountains, woodlands and forests, herds of red deer and, permeating all, an awareness that this is a countryside favoured by the presence of Royalty.

The village is pleasantly attractive, but not outstandingly so; it is the majestic surroundings that make it such a magnet for enthusiastic admirers of natural splendour. There are large hotels to cater for individual visitors and coach parties, a few shops and a scattering of bungalows and cottages, in one of which R. L. Stevenson wrote part of *Treasure Island*. The River Clunie rushes ecstatically between the buildings to share the joys of the Dee; spaciousness is provided by open greens. A nearby field is the venue of the games staged at the annual Highland Gathering, an event internationally famous.

Braemar is over a thousand feet above sea level but gives no impression of elevation; rather, it appears to be the floor of a great bowl formed by a ring of high mountains, a community inurned amongst sheltering heights.

Braemar across the valley

Below *River Dee near Braemar*

Braemar is an excellent centre for visitors, whether they come on wheels or on foot. Motorists who do not like to leave their cars, however, are restricted to the A.93 and a side road leading up the valley to the Linn of Dee, although Land-Rovers with permission may venture further. But this is primarily an area for strong walkers who can survive twenty or thirty rough miles in a day: a vast territory here awaits their exploration. In the winter months, the village is a convenient base for skiers.

Braemar is a threshold of the southern Cairngorms and it is to these fine mountains that most expeditions will be directed. Their southern aspect is incomparably more impressive than the northern from Aviemore, the mountains on this side appearing as well-defined individual peaks, not as an indefinite range. They are seen in full stature, some of their summits topping 4000 feet and many others coming near that figure. They are challenging, totally inhospitable, and have a loneliness and wildness that can be frightening and repelling in bad weather. These, in any conditions, are mountains for he-men.

The usual springboard for forays into the southern Cairngorms is the Linn of Dee, a well-known beauty spot reached by a side road from Braemar passing the cottages of Inverey; usually its environs are crowded by parked cars. Here the River Dee tumbles through a narrow rocky channel fringed by pines and spanned by the arch of a picturesque stone bridge. It is a lovely spot, ideal for a picnic. Many people intent on a long walk, have got no further than the Linn of Dee. Including me.

The Linn of Dee

THE SOUTHERN ASPECT

Linn of Dee is a starting point for the two great marathon walks across the Cairngorms, the Lairig Ghru (*see* p. 191) and the Lairig an Laoigh (*see* p. 196), aiming for Aviemore and Nethy Bridge respectively. They take the same route as far as Derry Lodge, reached by a private road from near the Linn, but there diverge to follow their own ways through the mountains. They are out of the question for walkers who have to return to cars parked at the Linn.

It is practicable, however, to get a foretaste of the Lairig Ghru by using the path thereto from Derry Lodge and crossing over into Glen Dee. There one leaves the path as it turns north up the valley of the Dee to a notch in the skyline far ahead, and takes another following the youthful Dee down-river to White Bridge, where a rough road leads in three miles to the Linn. This is an exhilarating walk of twelve miles with no serious climbing, no route-finding problems and no difficulties.

But by far the most rewarding short expedition from the Linn is the traverse of the ridge of Sgor Dubh and Sgor Mor, a modest elevation that gives a grandstand view of the southern Cairngorms. It is seen to perfection and in true perspective from this mid-height viewpoint, in my opinion the finest on the mainland for impressive mountain scenery. Both from Sgor Dubh and the higher Sgor Mor, the peaks are seen in splendid array and there are aerial views of the two Lairigs. Adding to the emotional impact on the senses is the awesome stillness of the scene: there is no movement, no sound, giving the onlooker the feeling that he is surveying a dead world.

The ridge extends from Glen Lui to Glen Dee, and the first height, Sgor Dubh, is attained by a rough and pathless scramble up the steep slope bordering Glen Lui on the west. It is then an easy walk along the wide ridge to the main summit, Sgor Mor, 2666 feet, which has intrinsic interest in its granite tors and potholes. Attention, however, will principally be directed to the classic view to the north, where the Dee has its beginnings amongst the highest peaks of the Cairngorms. Descent from Sgor Mor can be made directly to White Bridge, probably passing herds of grazing deer, for the return by road to Linn of Dee.

White Bridge

At White Bridge, the River Dee changes course, here taking its first chance to escape eastwards where its ultimate destiny lies.

Over the bridge, coming from Linn of Dee, two more long-distance walks start along a good track in unison as far as the Geldie Burn where a route to Glen Feshie turns alongside the stream into Glen Geldie, passing near some sad ruins that afford shelter; it continues over the Feshie watershed into Glen Feshie, going on to reach Strath Spey at Feshiebridge.

The other route is a more serious proposition. It crosses Geldie Burn and aims roughly south to a watershed and enters Glen Tilt and finally, after a thirty-mile journey, arrives at Blair Atholl on the A.9 after passing between the lonely mountains of the Forest of Atholl.

These two routes are clearly beyond the scope of anyone based on Braemar or who has to return to a car parked at the Linn of Dee, but both can be followed to their respective watersheds, then return-ing. The walk up Glen Geldie is simple and straightforward; that bound for Glen Tilt, although clear underfoot, is rougher, in confusing terrain, and should not be attempted in misty conditions. The watershed occurs five miles after leaving White Bridge, where from the little Loch Tilt (hidden from sight by an intervening ridge) issues the River Tilt to act as a perfect guide to Blair Atholl, still half a day's march distant.

I once ventured along the Glen Tilt path with my wife to photograph some of the mountains of the Forest of Atholl and to get a view down Glen Tilt, which I was able to do after scrambling to a heathery viewpoint above Loch Tilt, but I had wandered further than I intended and was already leg-weary as we turned to retrace our steps to White Bridge. I waded calf-deep across the Geldie Burn, too tired to search for a dry crossing, and at White Bridge stopped to empty the water out of my boots and have a rest and a smoke while my wife, much fitter than myself, went on to the Linn to wait for me in the car. I followed slowly, dragging my feet over the last three miles to the Linn. I had had more than enough. I should have had more sense. I was an advanced geriatric, and the seventeen miles I walked that day over rough ground was really too much for ancient legs. I am glad to report that I recovered after a good meal at Mar Lodge which at that time had recently opened a restaurant. Lesson: when you get to seventy, remember your age.

The mountains between Glen Geldie and Glen Tilt

Mar Lodge

WALKS FROM BRAEMAR

A long valley walk in the close company of the River Dee, and with beautiful views throughout, is available from Braemar. The road to Linn of Dee is taken, passing the picturesque waterfall of the Linn of Corriemulzie before reaching the cottages of Inverey. Over the bridge at Linn of Dee, a road on the north bank goes down-river to Mar Lodge, a spacious building, relatively modern and once used as a hotel and restaurant, also a centre for sporting activities. The road continues beyond, ending where the wooded ravine of Glen Quoich comes down from the hills to meet the Dee. A lane goes forward below heathery heights known as the Braes of Mar and is never far from the river. Across the water is Braemar, within shouting distance but inaccessible in the absence of a bridge, and the lane must be continued to the gracious Invercauld House, partly fifteenth century, where the A.93 can be joined at Invercauld Bridge for the return to Braemar.

Simple detours can be added by tireless walkers who consider eighteen miles a mere stroll, first by turning up Glen Ey at Inverey to see the chasm known as The Colonel's Bed and, secondly, by following a path leading up Glen Quoich to visit the Linn of Quoich where the descending stream flows over a bed of smooth slabs in a delightful setting.

Invercauld Bridge

Linn of Corriemulzie

Below *Linn of Quoich*

Another walk to be recommended to sojourners at Braemar leaves the A.93 two miles south of the village where a private road, open to walkers, turns left into Glen Callater and after three more miles arrives on the shore of Loch Callater with a splendid mountain prospect ahead. Nearby is Lochcallater Lodge from where Queen Victoria and the Prince Consort ascended Lochnagar on ponies. This is a simple walk in a quiet valley and the lochside is an ideal venue for an easy day.

But strong walkers may have set their sights on a longer expedition and, by continuing along the east side of the loch to the head of the valley and there following a rising path that climbs to and crosses the high plateau of Tolmount, a descent can be made into Glen Doll for Glen Clova. This is a route that calls for caution, especially on the confusing terrain of the Tolmount crossing where an absence of landmarks may cause steps to go astray in poor weather conditions. This is a fine walk but only if an overnight stay in Glen Doll, where there is a youth hostel, is planned, or if transport has been arranged to be waiting there for a return to Braemar by road. Failing this, if a return has to be made to Braemar on foot, it would be inadvisable to go further than Tolmount, visiting the summit of this shapely mountain as a consolation.

Loch Callater

Stalkers' ponies

Glen Doll is a short side valley turning off the head of Glen Clova, which carries the River South Esk down to the eastern coastal plain around Forfar and, being easy of access from the industrial fringe, is a popular place. There are imposing mountains around Glen Doll but the floor of the valley has been too severely afforested, destroying the natural grandeur of the scene. On the south side of the glen, the heights of Dreish and Mayar rise impressively above the treeline, the latter displaying a façade of cliffs a mile in length while the head is closed by the lofty skyline of Tolmount. There is a pedestrian escape to the north where an old packhorse road climbs over the Capel Mounth and descends to Glen Muick and Ballater (*see* p. 204), giving a possible route of return to Braemar if arrangements can be made for a car to be waiting at the Spittal of Muick car park. Walkers of only average ability, however, should confine their abilities to Glen Callater.

The path descending into Glen Doll from the Tolmount plateau is known as Jock's Road and a crude bothy by the side of the track was the scene of a tragic incident some years ago when a party of five young men were trapped here by bad weather and all died from exposure: there is a memorial plaque on a nearby rock. Jock's Road is notoriously difficult in mist or under snow. In good weather, the descent into Glen Doll is pleasant and interesting – until the plantations are reached.

A modern and aesthetically disturbing feature in the Highlands and especially noticeable in the Cairngorms is the bulldozing of rough roads along the mountainsides, these appearing as ugly scars visible for miles. Some in afforested areas, such as Glen Doll, are necessary for the removal of timber and in any case are hidden by trees. It is those that have scoured the heather and rocks from bare hillsides and penetrated quiet glens hitherto unspoiled that most offend the eye; these have the more sinister purpose of conveying sportsmen in Land-Rovers to their prey, bringing the victims within easier range of their guns. Such roads have largely supplanted the old stalkers' paths which were well graded, culverted and maintained in good condition: they were a joy to tread and fascinating to follow, and they were a boon to walkers, greatly easing passage through mountainous areas.

Many of the unobtrusive old tracks fashioned for men on foot and ponies will doubtless survive the further encroachment of bulldozers and jeeps. Time and weather will soften the harshness of the new roads but they will never replace in the affection of hillwalkers, the ladders to heaven provided by the man-made stalkers' paths.

The time has come to pack bags, say farewell to Braemar and head for home to resume the routine of everyday life. The A.93 awaits to point the way south, leaving the Highlands behind, but it provides a final thrill of excitement as it climbs the long incline up Glen Clunie to the top of the Cairnwell Pass, which deserves a last halt.

The Cairnwell Pass

THE CAIRNWELL PASS

The Cairnwell Pass has the highest motor road in Britain, having an altitude of 2109 feet, but it has earned a better claim to fame recently by the development here of popular ski grounds. The heights around are rounded and smooth and free of crags, hills rather than mountains although many exceed 3000 feet: they lack distinction and character and have little appeal to the hillwalker, but have proved ideal for ski runs. They are, moreover, within much easier reach of the populated south than the Aviemore district, making possible one-day visits without the need for overnight stays.

The scenery of the Cairnwell Pass is bleak and has no pretensions to beauty; the landscapes are harsh and austere. It is not a place to which visitors come to admire the surroundings, and less so now than ever because the development of skiing as a winter sport has led to the desecration of the neighbouring slopes by the installation of a chair-lift and ski-tows, with access paths, a large car park and a café.

The road over the pass descends to Glen Shee and the nature of the landscape changes: agricultural farmlands take the place of mountains, the animals seen grazing are cows, not red deer, the clarity of the atmosphere is gradually dulled as the road enters Blairgowrie and goes on to Perth.

The Cairnwell Pass, despite its bleakness, serves the itinerary well by providing a fitting finale, a last opportunity to look back at the Highlands from a mountaintop, a Munro that can be attained without physical effort. The dominant peak here is the Cairnwell itself, 3059 feet, and a chair-lift operates from the roadside to a point only a hundred yards from its stony summit.

The last mountain: Creag Leacach

My dislike of chair-lifts on mountains has lessened with advancing age, but I still think they offend the eye and inflict an indignity on noble mountains. The true satisfaction of climbing comes only after physical effort, not from being carried there. But perhaps by conveying the old and infirm to the high places they could never attain otherwise, such artificial aids have merit.

From the summit of the Cairnwell on a clear day, a wide panorama of the Highlands is seen, range after range of mountains extending to the far distance. Of the nearer heights, the one that most catches the eye is Creag Leacach, bordering the descent into Glen Shee.

Linger awhile. It is here we say a reluctant goodbye.

At the Glen Shee Sculpture Park

Returning by chair-lift down to the top of the pass, we enter the café and review the highlights of the journey over a cup of coffee, and then go across to the car park and turn the car to face south.

It is all over.

Home, James. Or, in my case, Home, Betty.

INDEX